Financialization
of
Daily Life

In the series
Labor in Crisis
edited by Stanley Aronowitz

Financialization
of
Daily Life

Randy Martin

 Temple University Press
PHILADELPHIA

Temple University Press, Philadelphia 19122
Copyright © 2002 by Temple University
All rights reserved
Published 2002
Printed in the United States of America

⊗ The paper used in this publication meets the requirements of
the American National Standard for Information Sciences—Permanence
of Paper for Printed Library Materials, ANSI Z39.48-1984

Library of Congress Cataloging-in-Publication Data

Martin, Randy.
    Financialization of daily life / Randy Martin.
        p.   cm.
    Includes bibliographical references and index.
    ISBN 1-56639-987-4 (cloth : alk. paper) — ISBN 1-56639-988-2 (pbk. :
alk. paper)
        1. Finance—United States. 2. Inflation (Finance)—United States.
    3. Cost and standard of living—United States. I. Title.

HG181 .M315 2002
332′.0973—dc21

                                                                2002020341

Contents

Acknowledgments

Financialization of Daily Life is about how credit and debt are lived. The book lives through healthy measures of both. In writing it, I have been happily encumbered by many productive exchanges. Stanley Aronowitz, Stefano Harney, and Toby Miller provided much appreciated insight. Peter Wissoker inspired the book at a delicious lunch. Micah Kleit provided a home at Temple, where the staff have been wonderful to work with. My own workplace, Tisch School of the Arts at New York University, has been a most supportive environment. Mary Schmidt Campbell, the dean with whom I work, is inspirational. Anita Dwyer and Michelle Davidson are tremendous office collaborators who make it possible to be both an administrator and a writer. Theresa Smalec afforded remarkable research assistance, turning up reams of material I could not have imagined existed. Mario Motti is my dear financialization poster child. Ginger Gillespie, Oliver, and Sophia give me much to come home to. These are the debts that I can never have enough of.

Financialization
of
Daily Life

Introduction

What in the World Is Financialization?

"Suddenly, finance is fun." This from a full-page ad for WingspanBank.com, another of the myriad Internet startups bent on sparing no effort to convince the reader to embrace a "new way" in financial services.[1] The visual in the ad is of two naked infants, one black, one white, gazing upon a computer screen emblazoned with the Wingspan logo. Though we cannot see their facial expressions, we come to the image of the future through their innocent attentions. The arm of the black child rests snugly upon the shoulder of a white companion whose tuft of hair suggests infant femininity precociously lent support by her man. A new breed of financial services customer? A couple who grow up banking together? A bank for a multicultural future where there is no redlining in cyberspace? A friendly interface so simple and secure that it reduces financial self-management to child's play? A rival to television's claims on the kids' affections? Many are the possibilities. The ad copy under the youngsters' pristine bottoms provides a few more clues. "The old way was hard. The new way is easy. Now you can search the nation for a better mortgage without leaving the den. Check your investments. Find better car insurance. Even plan the kids' education at 11:15 P.M. and still be there for

1

their midnight bottle. Can your bank do that? Would they if they could?"

And so it is the parent's amusement the new way augurs. Round-the-clock vigilance to support the family can now be embraced with ease. The future can be made secure by constant improvement of present household finance. No parent should rest until new rates have been found. What the front door of the home once left behind is now invited into that paramount relaxation center—the den—via electrical outlet and telephone jack. What once belonged to the workaday world beds down with leisure and domesticity. Advertised here is not simply a different way to bank, but a new way of life. Precise time-allocations, clear-minded calculations, uninterrupted self-control, unceasing escalation of output— these are no longer just the tokens of career success, but of domestic bliss. So, just where is the pleasure in finance? Wherein lies the novelty that is so suddenly ours?

Perhaps it's a bit silly to take a single ad so seriously— or literally. The kinds of claims it makes are certainly not unique. More pointedly, Wingspan's life as a distinct entity was typically brief, just over a year before it was assimilated into the electronic operations of giant BankOne.[2] At the crest of the 1990s boom, when Wingspan and its ilk appeared, the prophets of a new day were legion. Economists told us that business cycles were a thing of the past. Wall Street gurus proclaimed that stock prices could rise indefinitely. Internet avatars squealed with technophilic delight of humanity rescued through infinite communication. Globalization promoters informed us that finance made the world one. No doubt much is conflated and confused in these grand claims, and little is contested in the promise that the new ways are good for us all. The loud chant of new times—heard even after markets tumbled and new economics faltered—can drown out historical continuities and restrain more complicated appraisals of social context. When novelty comes suddenly, it is as if it has been already embraced and assimilated. Sorting out what is different, where changes have come from, what is still with us, and what has taken a turn for the worse complicates the present and adds options to the ways in which life might be lived. Money has long commanded the attention of all who would be forced to survive its whimsy or to profit by its movement. In a market economy, money is both the means and ends of life. But the present invitation to live by finance—which has survived the fizzled boom—is still being extended to players beyond the corporate world. A financially leavened existence asks for different measures of participation in shaping the values of polity and economy than did earlier challenges posed by market life. Finance, the management of money's ebbs and flows, is not simply in the service of accessible wealth, but presents itself as a merger of business and life cycles, as a means for the acquisition of self. The financialization of daily life is a proposal for how to get ahead, but also a medium for the expansive movements of body and soul. Any proposition as ambitious as this is bound to get unruly. Once all the features are unpacked, the nature of this self-in-the-making may turn out to be far from secure. Before assuming the integrity of a new market syndrome, it pays to look closely at the symptoms and sort out the familiar and the strange. In this respect, what Wingspan had on offer is symptomatic of the changing face of a complex syndrome—as curious as it is unexceptional.

Advertising a New Dream

Wingspan promised nothing less than a new corporate culture for a different kind of consumer. Their web site spoke of a different way of doing business, much the way the Saturn automobile manufacturer advertises its enlightened labor relations. The expertise and information are free for the asking and always available. Instead of a board of directors, a demotic band of advisers just like the good reader run the show at Wingspan. "The iBoard is made up of a diverse group of everyday women and men who realize the potential of on-line banking. These are not stuffed-shirt executives. As a part of our promise to be what your bank would be if it could start over, we invited users from all across the country to be a part of the iBoard. They know what it's like to stand in long bank lines, and know firsthand what it's like to deal with pushy salespeople selling insurance, mortgages, investments, and other financial products. And they know there is a better way to bank."[3]

These few stand in for the bureaucratic suffering of the many. On closer inspection, the parallel to Saturn is well placed. Like its car cousin, Wingspan was never a scrappy start-up but a subsidiary of a market leader, in this case First USA Bank Corporation, among the largest issuers of credit cards in the United States. While Saturn is folksy enough to listen to its workers, it's also corporate enough to pay them less than workers at other divisions of parent company General Motors are paid. Boasting "the world's first virtual advisory board of directors," Wingspan offered a disclaimer about these advisers that while it may value their opinions, "there is no legal obligation for the bank to accept their advice or otherwise be held responsible for their actions." Is this the old routine of bait and switch? Lure them in with a pitch to the democratic vox populi and then show them who's really boss? Or is this really a statement of how the customers should understand their newfound powers of round-the-clock participation? The Internet bank devoted to maximizing its customers' "financial potential" and escaping the "pitfalls" of conventional banks "where you can manage almost every significant aspect of your financial life" wants to gently suggest that the risk as well as the money is ours to keep.

In the end, Wingspan offered little that could not be found from the electronic services of the "brick and mortar" banks to which it proclaimed itself the alternative. From the perspective of the conventional banks, the firewall between them and their virtual varieties is also strategic—an effort to avoid an internecine battle for their own customer base and employees, a threat known as cannibalization. According to one senior bank executive, "We understand cannibalization; if you don't do it yourself, it will eventually come from outside."[4] And so Wingspan was eaten by its owner. Interest on checking accounts, on-line bill payment, investment advice, and financial planning tools are bundled together the way a reinvented Amazon.com has devoured rain forests of hitherto disparate inventory. The difference lies in the didactic functions. Most electronic merchandisers assume their users are already hooked on shopping and responsive to point and click directives. Somehow, the visual attachments of virtual surfing have nestled in the pleasure zones once thought to reside with the touch and feel of store-bought commodities.

The financial planning bug is a different worm to catch than the nearly extinct species called savings. Savings rested upon a mass psychology of deferred gratification, putting off the pleasure of expenditure today for a rewarding tomorrow. The twist in Wingspan's marketing of planning is that the self-managed life will be freed from its Puritan past to turn life into an endless business school course where, finally, education is fun because the teacher has been banished. In the new psychology, money is not to be left untouched, but constantly fondled, mined daily like a well-stocked refrigerator.

Clearly there is money to be made by firms when their customers do work once performed by their employees. The rampaging mergers and acquisitions in financial services have cast out both brand names and thousands of jobs once thought to be secure. The most aggressive of these, like the amalgamation of Citicorp and Travelers Insurance to form Citigroup, present a more ambitious bundling of activities than that offered by Wingspan. Tellingly, while Wingspan was assimilated, Travelers is to be spun off as a separate subsidiary. Much separates initial claims from subsequent practice. Some continuities are emerging. The integration of financial services augurs a new orientation of monetary affairs in the life of the individual of means.

Like every prior incarnation of the good life, this one rests as much upon exclusion as inclusion. An unprecedented 50 percent of the population in the United States partakes of some form of stock market investment. This figure is roughly the proportion of registered voters who joined in the last several presidential elections and corresponds as well to the ratio of households who have purchased a personal computer. As a household appliance denoting a certain status, the initial marketing of this box for domestic computation (like balancing checkbooks) failed until it was reinvented as a communications device by means of the Internet. The Internet is already a studied conflation of work and leisure, priceless freedom and commerce. From this perspective, it is the perfect portal to financialize daily life. Yet even here, less than 5 percent of on-line activity is accounted for by households doing their banking, and just over 15 percent of time on-line is taken up with equity trades—although 70 percent of individuals who trade use the net.[5] As growth in the sales of computers is expected to decline within the United States in the years ahead, investors are banking on increasing sales through e-commerce, rather than extending access. Being plugged in is less a function of whether computers are affordable, for the prices of the machines have tumbled as they have been marketed as handsets for service providers in the same way that telephones are. The built-in limitation is not whether someone has something to communicate, but whether the person has a portfolio to manage. From this perspective, it is unsurprising that patterns of Internet use would follow the concentration of wealth in the United States.

In global terms, the financial subject that Wingspan imagined is a far cry from the universal ambitions of the Enlightenment's thinking being. For all its democratic trappings and intended global reach, the new life is not being designed with the same capaciousness as the prior models of consumer paradise. This is not to say that the previous incarnation of the good life did not also rest upon exclusions, ones that divided the nation along lines of race and gender that limited where one could work, live, and gain union representation.

Capitalism prides itself on wealth making. The social question is what to make of that wealth. Beyond making a slim percentage fat, what impact did the financially driven expansion have on what are taken as typical habits of life? We can judge capital's reign not only by the riches and misery it produces, but also by its own promise to enrich the way we are together. True, the U.S. economy blasted through prior records of sustained expansion, but only after years of growth did wages for the least affluent begin to creep up and reverse a twenty-five-year period of decline. A stingy result to such unprecedented wealth creation. When the expansion sprang a leak just after the new millennium dawned and wage growth fizzled while unemployment began to rise, it was easy to speculate that even this modest wealth sharing was considered excessive by the architects of the new economy. More people in the work force putting in more time. So who's going to go to the bank? And how to make sure that the added homework is fun and not the butt of jokes? Above all, how to assess the social impact of such wealth creation—what changes in the theory and practice of the good life did all that money buy? Understanding financialization entails more than tracking new disequalities and distributions; it entails probing the new logics by which strange customs are made to feel normal. This is going to take some learning.

The Coin of a Realm

Financialization, like those other recently minted conceptual coins postmodernism and globalization, gets stretched and pulled in myriad directions. Part of the complexity of these terms is that they stand simultaneously as subject and object of analysis—something to be explained and a way of making sense out of what is going on around us. These are also words meant to capture the novelty of the moment with an exuberance that can make us lose sight of longer historical processes of which they are a part. Insofar as these terms are meant to reference some change that is afoot, they demonstrate how things thought to be stable and fixed in their places are actually in dynamic motion. Self–society, local–global, private–public, economics–politics, reason–unreason, decisions based on information and risk based on uncertainty are key distinctions for understanding our world. Yet a proper understanding of financialization should show us how such fundamental distinctions depend upon the opposite member of each particular couplet at the same time that something beyond each of these dualistic pairs is alluded to.

To be useful to any comprehensive understanding of a complex world, financialization must refer to many different processes at once. The different dynamics would seem to operate apart from each other, but the burden of a useful analysis is to show how they work together. How individuals come to think about themselves, take stock of how they are doing and what they have accomplished, and how they know themselves to be moving forward through the measured paces of finance, yields a particular subjectivity. The sociologist Max Weber suggested as much when he referred to the "calculating attitude" needed to affirm that one's life deeds amounted to a fulfillment of one's calling. Such persons would prize a life lived by rules that resulted in a clear accumulation of the results of one's efforts. This he called the spirit of capitalism. Financialization as both subjectivity and moral code assumes that capitalism has been dispirited and profaned. This assumption is not meant to suggest that capitalism is about to expire. Weber wanted to know how a market-driven society could emerge from an ethos that seemed at odds with profit for its own sake. The spiritual quest to answer a calling became blind secular ambition, an attribute today taken as axiomatic to the winding road of virtually any career trajectory.

Financialization promises a way to develop the self, when even the noblest of professions cannot emit a call that one can answer with a lifetime. It offers a highly elastic mode of self-mastery that channels doubt over uncertain identity into fruitful activity. It insinuates the fertile mind in a labyrinth of rules that channel and contain vistas overwrought with information. Paths to action with definable results that clearly distinguish good from bad in measurable terms of success and failure are provided when it seemed that nothing could be done. This is not to say that financialization occupies all the room of the self or monopolizes the ethical domain, but that its medium and its message make themselves known and heard above the din.

If the protocols of a financially intelligent and meaningful life were simply options freely chosen, we could say that at least some people had voted with their own feet to embrace the new way as the corpse of the old was buried. The instruments of persuasion are more than just newspaper ads and television spots. When financialization is examined as official policy, the rhetoric that invites us to embrace the new gets tangled up with an assassination of the older set of expectations for how citizens should relate to society and what they should demand of their government. In this regard, it suggests a new or revised social contract both for the corporate welfare states that once fit the moniker First World and as model of developmental decorum for those nations grouped as Third World.

As people around the world can attest, refusal or inability to take up the new social contract has punishing effects no less violent than the coercive forces that made and sustained colonies and empires. Then as now such historical innovations have their velvet gloves, adorned with beautiful embroidery that reads "civilization" and "progress." As one-size-fits-all accessories, these terms have become frayed and faded. Financialization makes a noble attempt to adhere economic movement to the passage of time in a way that progress once did. The usual suspects of reason, efficiency, and freedom are rounded up to testify on its behalf. It remains the case, however, that all the wealth marshaled under the sign of finance's advance in the past few decades (and the long charge of the 1990s especially) has failed to garner the widespread optimism and enthusiasm of prior incarnations of prosperity. It is hard to say that this is simply a failure of distributive mechanisms and that some tinkering with tax codes or tithes will make the people happy again. The capitalist juggernaut careened past its checkpoints and goalposts, beyond its own wildest expectations. Yet having met its mission, a new sense of project is harder to fix with any degree of confidence. Pleasures abound, but it is not clear that they can deliver the fun promised by the older models.

Perhaps part of the disconnect between societal means and ends thought to be so intricately harmonized by finance lies in the difficulty it encounters in reckoning its own success. Economic fundamentals—measurements of growth, inflation, productivity, unemployment, consumer confidence, money supply—become flustered under the financial gaze. As a new package of principles of political economy, financialization may not have been given due time to ripen intellectually before it was taken out of the box. Here too, however, confusion is invited by the myriad of referents. A use of money, extension of credit, or state of indebtedness can make it possible to purchase or produce something not currently within one's means. But finance is also the industry that organizes these activities and introduces its own innovations in product lines and services so that the possessive relations between persons and things are dissolved and reassembled.

The connections forged when pieces of ownership are reassigned, such as the bundling of individual deeds to homes into mortgage-backed securities, transcend the immediacies of place and physically bounded community. The usefulness of such commodities has to do with how they allow for further exchange. If these products are to find their market, demand has to be identified and promoted where there was thought to be none, legislation will have to be redrafted, and somewhere links of need and want will get pulled in different directions. Financialization integrates markets that were separate, like banking for business and consumers, or markets for insurance and real estate. It asks people from all walks of life to accept risks into their homes that were hitherto the province of professionals. Without significant capital, people are being asked to think like capitalists. Diversified interests may wind up soliciting curious forms of self-interest, particularly if individuals need to begin thinking through so many other selves. Ironically, just when life seemed to be tailored so that rational actors could make decisions with perfect access to information, the rules for how to conduct one's business, for what could count as information, and for ways of addressing oneself to it became so complex as to mess up the equation all over again. The challenge of financialization is to consider what fresh and hitherto unrecognizable ways of intervening in and shaping the world get opened up in the process.

1 Too Much of a Good Thing?

The world is awash in money. Thirty trillion dollars changes hands in a month. Well, actually, hands rarely get into the picture. Most money is transferred from account to account electronically. Wealth can ricochet around the globe like a bullet, but never sear the flesh. While many are untouched, few are unaffected. The United States broke its own records for economic growth during the 1990s. The same could not be said for the rest of the world, where poverty and development remained for many an internecine conflict.[1] The expansion in the United States was initially unable to deliver much more than rising inequality for four-fifths of *its* population.[2] Yet, by the middle of the decade, not only were those in middle-income brackets seeing their incomes rise, but even those at the bottom of the income distribution were being positively affected by the sustained prosperity.

At the end of the decade and the beginning of the 2000 election year, the annual report issued by the president's Council of Economic Advisers offered a rosy view of what the decade's expansion had delivered to the citizenry. The report provided an easy key to what continued growth meant. Each successive generation would see living standards double every thirty-five years, something that could be experienced within one's own lifetime. These projections of hope assumed that the average growth rate of 2.5 percent that prevailed over the past one hundred years would continue in the future and that the rising inequality of the prior twenty-five years would abate.[3]

Whether or not such projections pan out, the relationship between growth and standard of living is more tenuous still. Assuming that a growth rate for the economy as a whole can be distributed among a population merely by dividing one number into another simply states the problem of how to translate quantity into quality. It is understandable why people might not perceive that they are indeed doing better. The numerical comparisons are made over time, and a sense of well-being is formed in the moment. Rather than a sense of success, disappointment reigns. The hard facts of the economy don't translate into experience in the way in which the economists might expect. The experts wield the mantle of objectivity against misinformed subjective states on the expectation that the information will correct the ill-gotten impression that money is not doing what it should be doing for people. Money may be many things—medium of exchange, store of value, measure of equivalence—but it also presents a standard that cannot be met.

The economic boom of the 1990s presents an opportunity to understand what increasing wealth failed to deliver. The boom occurred without a generalized sense of expansion that seemed to be its rightful inheritance on the basis of past economic upturns. At first this lack would seem merely to be a problem of inadequately equitable distribution of economic gain, a correction for which is easy to propose, albeit difficult to achieve. When some tempering of inequality did occur, little celebration was heard. If the relation between growth and well-being is so freighted, what beyond shifting inequality is at issue? Is there a deeper shift in how the financial correlates of prosperity are lived?

The figures for growth that these economists use is what they call real growth, an increase in the total value of goods and services produced per year, controlled for inflation, which is a rise in the price of those same products. The economic expansions of the 1950s and 1960s had higher rates of growth (together averaging more than 4 percent), but by the end of the century, the lower rate was treated as the more virtuous one, because it was taken to be noninflationary. One could appreciate how economists working for a president who had come to office remembering something called "the economy" would be careful to present the existing state of affairs as the best conceivable one. Their predictions for the sustainability of good times for the economy proved no better than those for their party's electoral prospects. Yet Albert Gore Jr.'s fate in the 2000 presidential election bore some resemblance to the fate of the economy —as people could come to see and live it. Gore's superior numbers (he wound up with half a million more tallied votes than his rival—and this number says nothing of the excluded Floridians) could not win him the election. Likewise, the economic prosperity indexed by the numbers did not seem to translate into a winning mood for the populace.

Other numbers, poll results, collected over the decade suggested that people did not believe that prosperity was theirs. Majorities felt the "American Dream" impossible; minorities held that the "good life" could be theirs. While real inflation may have been under control, the imagined cost to support the good life had skyrocketed, from $50,000 to $100,000 from the end of the 1980s to the middle of the 1990s.[4] Why couldn't people see the truth of the economy?

Was it because they weren't paying attention to the numbers, or was their doubt the price they paid for their attentions? What might account for the apparent disconnect between measures of the economy's objectivity and the people's subjectivity? With information pertaining to finance more abundant than ever, could this disconnection be a feature of economic life, a way of living it, rather than a neglect of evidence? And if so many shared this disconnection, was it a disconnection at all or rather an unexpected, awkward, and uneasy way in which people were brought into contact with one another by an emerging kind of understanding?

The ascent of finance cannot be explained simply in terms of an accumulation of wealth, from which perspective it is by no means novel (those with money always seem to gain the upper hand). The present predominance of finance needs to be seen as something that brings people together only to seem to take away what they thought they possessed. Hence, while seeming to operate with no hands at all, the magic of finance is its ability to take by giving, to spread growth while denying to those who might partake of it the very wealth it puts in view. This too is a familiar tale of society where the concentration of wealth passes as a spectacle for all to enjoy, even as most suffer being dispossessed of it. Stars, for example, are eye candy, publicly displayed private lives for the vicarious, visual, and collective consumption of wealth. Perhaps this observation helps explain reports of ambivalence rather than resentment toward inequality.[5]

The current financial mode is not simply spectacle, an eye-catching economic view, but an invitation to participate in what is on display as a fundamental part of oneself. Finance is not only the question of what to do with the money one has worked for, but a way of working that money over, and ultimately, a way of working over oneself. With the new model of financial self-management, making money does not stop with wages garnered from employment. Money must be spent to live, certainly, but now daily life embraces an aspiration to make money as well. These are opportunities that quickly have obligations to invest wisely, speculate sagely, and deploy resources strategically. The market is not only a source of necessary consumables; it must be beaten. To play at life one must win over the economy.

When personal finance becomes the way in which ordinary people are invited to participate in that larger abstraction called the economy, a new set of signals are introduced as to how life is to be lived and what it is for. It would be naive to think that these signals obliterate other messages from other sources or are without noise and confusion. There has always been a dilemma for those seeking to understand how societies characterized by disequalities of wealth, such as this one, persist. In the simplest terms, why would people put up with a situation in which the rich get richer and the poor poorer? If the means that people use to get through their days invite them to believe that such states of affairs are necessary or even immutable, why would people believe in ideas that are, in a sense, bad for them? Rather than being left with the unsavory notion that those who would be the ordinary heroes of history might be so readily duped or doped (while those who might study these folk and speak on their behalf had the good fortune to be inoculated against bad ideas), attention was increasingly paid to how societies oriented toward the gain of the few nonetheless created processes of participation for the multitude.

These opportunities for participation had real costs that seemed to belie the narrow self-interest of those in command, but were intended to secure lifetime allegiance that linked personal betterment to economic growth.

The preferred example here is Henry Ford, who in 1914 had the better idea of paying his employees what was then the whopping sum of $5 a day. By paying higher labor costs than his competitors, Ford appeared to undercut himself. Instead, he aimed to forge a caste of workers who could afford to purchase the products they produced. Of course, Ford's workers wouldn't simply exchange their paychecks for a Model T; they would need credit to acquire a vehicle. To be creditworthy, workers would have to be able to account for where they could be found, not only in the present, but also in the future. It would help to have a permanent address tied to lifelong employment at a predictable level of income. These would come together in home ownership. The home could secure long-term credit and debt and also be an object of further finance. Ford's model workers would also need a firm conviction that the thing they labored over by day could serve them at night, that they should invest in their own futures, that tomorrow was a brighter day.

This is the apocryphal tale of the emergence of consumerism as the American Dream, also known as Fordism. While Ford's vision was long on exclusions (especially of women and minorities), tolerant of Fascism, and intolerant of the very pleasures typically associated with the consumerist ethos, the faiths he preached are now seen to have fallen on hard times.[6] The fixed commitments to the social life of the worker have been traded in for flexibilities in employment, residence, and consumables—where the customized is now to be considered king. The flight from Ford's fantasy of the good life is more paradoxical than any simple shift from, say, industrial to service economy could capture.

Finance is key. Consumer credit and debt have been extended beyond the wildest imaginings of their architects in the 1920s. One consequence is a historic high of home ownership—two-thirds of households in the United States by the end of the twentieth century, an increase of almost 50 percent over what the rate had been a hundred years earlier.[7] And certainly, more consumables clutter these homes than ever before. While new homes themselves have acquired a third more square footage since 1970, even poor households have seen acquisitive gains.[8] More hours need to be put in by more people to pay these debts. It would seem less that consumerism had come to an end as a practice, than that it has been realized for so many as a way of life that it can no longer serve as a vision of what might be. While the improvements associated with acquisition of these material goods cannot be discounted, it is impossible to return to the past to enjoy the difference. More pointedly, it is unclear what in the present would orient people to the gains of this acquisition. When a dream is lived, it is a dream no longer.

Perhaps the same might be said of Fordism as well. What appeared to rely on an industrial separation between work and home, one that came, interestingly, when service jobs, not manufacturing jobs, were overtaking the farm as the center of work in America, in practice aimed to establish production and consumption on parallel tracks of well-defined discipline and efficiency. On this view, financialization would be Fordism brought home, not so much as gainful self-employment (albeit tied to a boss's or client's modem), but as the fully realized labor of consumption. But this reckoning, while refusing any clean break between past and present, leaves too much intact.

What it means to own something, just like what it means to be possessed of oneself, undergoes significant modulation under financialization. The securitization of consumer debt, the bundling of individual bills into bonds that can be traded in specialized markets, spreads ownership around in vexing ways. More profoundly, and elusively, the Fordist dream for Americans prescribed a clear separation between present and future. To be a dreamscape, tomorrow had to be different from today in describable terms that could be saved for, but also indescribably different in ways that would allow the future to assume the aspiration and desire that make dreaming possible in the first place. It is in this area that the emergence of rather droll monetary policy, specifically the priority to control inflation through regulation of interest rates by the Federal Reserve Board, can be associated with far more extensive experiential consequences. It is in the intimate but highly mediated links between what amounts to a different governmental disposition toward its own regulatory activity and those it governs that the ascent of finance must be traced.

Governing Finance

Now that the twentieth century is over, its story can be told. Markets are supposed to run themselves. The invisible hand is morally pure, like the Victorian household, not because it is free from coercive machinations, but because such devices of regulation remain unseen and opaque from without. Privatization is not merely the sell-off of public assets and services to profit-seeking enterprises, but a purgation of the morally sullied public figured in and as government. The triumph of the market entails the defeat of the idea of communism abroad and the idea of government at home as the twinned dragons that fetter economic liberation.

The greatest fable of twentieth-century economics is the passage from Keynesian to monetarist truths about the ways of the world. On the one hand, this is a shift from public opinion and policy concern over labor's negative condition—unemployment—to that of capital—inflation. Along the way, the priority given to including workers fully in the labor market yields to the primacy of the investor as the way to orient domestic policy and ideas of citizenship. But for polite company, this is the story of culture yielding to nature, of artificial state intervention coming to terms with the organic rhythms of market law. It is the promise to "get government off our backs," "to end government as we know it," mouthed by presidents from both parties. Of course, the rise of monetarism as governing creed belies this narrative in practice even as it is celebrated as triumphant. For monetarism to succeed on its own terms requires massive government intervention and mounting regulatory mechanisms. Unemployment remains a key trigger of government actions, but now as an anxiety that too few are out of work and increased demand will raise wages and foment inflation, which in turn discourages investment. This is in contrast to the Keynesian concern that when too many are out of work, aggregate demand is weakened and goods go unsold.

Government regulation extends way beyond legislation passed by Congress and signed into law by the president. Guidelines and regulations of various stripes can be promulgated directly by executive order, a handy device especially when legislative agendas may be deadlocked in a partisan-divided congress. All these are incorporated into the 150,000-page Code of Federal Regulations. One economist, Brian Goff, has come up with an index of federal regulations that includes pages in the Federal Register, the ratio of lawyers to the general population, the number of state employees, and the ratio of civil to criminal court cases. Growth in this index takes off after 1970 and continues through Republican and Democratic administrations alike.[9]

Keynesian economics emerged from concern over social unrest prompted by the failures of the market during the Great Depression to provide growth and employment opportunities. Government would prime the pump, or stimulate demand for production and therefore create employment, through expenditures on goods and services that individuals could not purchase. These would range from military material (and the wars that created demand for it) to social services for the poor. Hence, hawkish foreign policy came together with the creation of entitlements to basic human services (and the professionals and institutions who could provide these).

Keynesian initiatives were most strongly associated with Democratic administrations and eras—Franklin Roosevelt's New Deal, Lyndon Johnson's Great Society—but Richard Nixon's first term policies started down a similar path. They did at least until war came home, growth faltered, and inflation swelled. By 1973, with recession to hand, U.S. command over international financial arrangements (enshrined as the Bretton Woods accords in 1944 by John Maynard Keynes himself) was shattered, and the dollar no longer served to anchor the value of the rest of the world's currency. The dollar would regain its sovereignty as an instrument of currency exchange, but without the same connotation that its value would be met on demand by the U.S.

government. International currency exchange rates would float, and the hands that propped up the dollar bill would appear invisible. Dollars that had circulated in support of international business dealings left significant deposits around the world, especially in Europe. Companies could promise payment to each other, and these notes could be bonded in U.S. currency held in foreign banks (Eurodollars). Bonds, securities, and other denominated agreements to issue credit and repay debt expanded precipitously in this climate.

The rise in inflation had a similarly disruptive effect on the perceptions of those consumer institutions designed for the accumulation of future funds, namely, banks. A fixed-interest-rate certificate of deposit lost much of its charm when the rate of inflation exceeded what was advertised as a return by the bank. The mutual fund would emerge as the alternative savings instrument, and with it, the ascendance of investment banking. To bring investment banking into the realm of consumer activity, in 1975 the Securities and Exchange Commission would repeal fixed commissions for stockbrokers, thereby abetting the rise of discount brokerage houses (those that only sold stock, and did not finance new stock offerings of companies going public). Deregulation of financial services was oriented toward creating a consumer rather than business face for stock ownership.[10] The expansion of global and domestic financial transactions reflected in these developments saw financial assets surpass those of the production economy by 1973.[11] While financial capital was expanding, it was assisted by a reorientation of governmental regulation of the economy. The limits to industrially based growth were captured by the term *stagflation* and embodied in the presidency of Jimmy Carter. For Carter, the limits to growth were not only economic, but also ethical and ecological. His watchword was balance rather than prosperity. The flight from government activism—or at least the disbelief in the ameliorative effects of government intervention after Vietnam, left open the door to a far more conservative policy impulse. If there were real limits to what governments could do, then how can one justify tax bills? In short order, taxes themselves would come to be painted as denying economic mobility, as "income tax creep" pushed people into higher brackets that only left them poorer.

Such at least were the arguments of the domestic policy advocates of monetarism. Government should be in the business of stimulating supply not demand, and it could do so by increasing income through tax cuts. New York congressman Jack Kemp anointed himself standard-bearer of this supply-side economics, and the Kemp-Roth bill cutting tax rates was passed in 1977, with others soon to follow. But, in 1979, it was Carter himself who appointed Paul Volcker, a confirmed monetarist, to head the Federal Reserve Board as the nation's chief of monetary supply. Of course, governments can affect the supply of money by printing it, but far more of the magnitude of money in circulation comes from the pens of businesses, not from government presses. Rather than spending money on social goods to stimulate economic activity, the monetarist approach is to set interest rates by which money is lent to banks (the prime rate) to either stimulate investment or curtail it (if inflation may loom). Because interest rates are set hierarchically, keyed to this government's prime rate, the actions of government retain their centrality in the regulatory process.

A presidential appointee that straddles the electoral cycle, the central banker is not an elected official. The renewable four-year terms are meant to present this mode of regulation as outside of politics. The careful attention given to what the Fed does and says insinuates state action in the daily activities of the market. The ballooning bond market initiated in the 1980s introduced the prospect of all manner of novel financial instruments. Prominent among these are derivatives, promissory notes extracted from and therefore linked to another underlying asset, and the securitization of otherwise nonsalable debts, like home mortgages and automobile loans, into tradable assets. Around two-thirds of home mortgages are securitized in this manner. Between 1980 and the mid-1990s, new bond issues grew from 3.3 percent to 14.8 percent of GDP.[12] By 1994, the issues of derivatives were valued at more than $15 trillion.

While the bond market is greater than the one for stocks, ownership is far more concentrated. While nearly half of U.S. households own some stock (and the wealthiest tenth own four-fifths of all stock), by 1995 only 3 percent of households owned bonds.[13] The high-risk, high-rolling hedge funds that speculated in derivatives were indemnified against government oversight by a 1996 securities law exempting funds with fewer than 500 "owners." By protecting this ground against regulation, the government's action promoted the formation of highly exclusive funds with very high minimums. In the case of Long Term Capital Management (LTCM), the hedge fund whose initial successes gave credence to the complex mathematical models developed by its Nobel Prize–winning directors Robert C. Merton and Myron Scholes, $10 million was the price of entry. When this elite entity took its terrible fall in 1998, it was Alan Greenspan who assembled the private banks to broker a bailout.

One could say that Greenspan has long been in the business of legitimating the risks of wealth, whether he held a government post or not. On the eve of his appointment as chair of the Federal Reserve, Greenspan penned a letter to the Federal Home Loan Bank in San Francisco on February 13, 1985, at the request of Charles Keating—a notorious figure in what would become the Savings and Loan debacle to come. For this note, Keating's Lincoln Savings was declared to pose "no foreseeable risk" to the regulatory agency that insures deposits, the Federal Savings and Loan Corporation, and Greenspan was paid $40,000. Greenspan was endorsing Keating's plans to use federally insured deposits to purchase Michael Milken's junk bonds. The use of government action to protect finance entails this double action of exemption and bailout, evident for both Lincoln Savings and LTCM.[14] In both cases, it is the expansion of new markets for financial products that is being abetted—necessarily—by those very voices proclaiming the state to be unneeded for the expansion of wealth.

This irony has been nowhere clearer than with Alan Greenspan's public pronouncements at the Fed, words that were taken as instrumental to volatility in the price of stocks. While changes in interest rates are Fed actions of last resort, semiotic releases can occur daily in the form of speeches, congressional testimony, or meetings of the board. These pronouncements were meant to be prophetic.[15] Other kinds of state action need to be identified to grasp the ascent of finance. One is the use of discretionary spending. For all the talk of supply-side economics curtailing government's role in the economy, the size of the federal budget doubled during the 1980s, and the annual deficit and accumulated debt expanded mightily. The red ink was spilled by cutting taxes and increasing military expenditures. It has been said that the deficits were strategic, and meant to preempt demand for any further entitlements on the grounds that these would be budget breaking. Insofar as popular demands might translate into new allocations for emerging social needs, the answer was "Just say no." In practice, discretionary spending as a percentage of GDP remained relatively constant at 10 percent during the Reagan years. It was President Bill Clinton who significantly reduced the proportion of the nation's wealth spent this way, and it was he who realized the letter (if not always the spirit) of the supply-sider's creed.[16] During the Clinton years, discretionary spending dropped from 9 percent to 6 percent of GDP.[17]

Legislation meant to signal the intent to reduce deficits had been put in place during the mid-1980s, with the Gramm-Rudman-Hollings bill, the Balanced Budget and Emergency Deficit Control Act of 1985, and the Gramm-Rudman legislation of 1987, which required in the course of planning that expenditures in one area be offset by cuts or tax increases in another. These bills did not provide remedies for actual deficits because they only mandated projections within target ranges of expenditure. They did, however, set a tone for future legislation, like the Budget Enforcement Act of 1990, that implemented constant budgetary correction through pay-as-you-go surveillance.

While Clinton visibly failed to enact health-care coverage, quieter success was achieved in deficit reduction and shifting expenditure to the states, most notably through devolution of welfare costs. The public perception that Clinton supported increased entitlements seemed only to assist in achieving their curtailment. Other discretionary items like military expenditure were also kept at bay, as mergers of defense contractors were encouraged (as in the case of Lockheed-Martin) and some conversion to private welfare services took place. As deficits shrank, so too did the percentage of the federal budget that went toward interest payments. Modest tax increases in the early 1990s (in the larger context of reduced tax loads for the wealthy) meant that as wealth concentrated in the highest tax brackets, government would receive higher revenues, ultimately resulting in budget surpluses. As new appropriations became a smaller share and entitlements a larger share of the federal budget, less money was available for discretionary spending. Federal revenues grew from 18.2 percent of GDP in 1990 to 20.5 percent of GDP in 1998.[18] Clinton had made good on the supply-side claims to free wealth (in his terms "grow the economy") in a way that ultimately contributed to federal revenues. He furthered the new legislation (known as deregulation) needed to promote the realignment of commercial and consumer finance, most notably the elimination of the 1933 Glass-Steagall Act through the Financial Services Act of 1999.

The trends regarding the number of public laws passed during the Clinton years are worth noting here, especially in light of the constraints placed on such action by what came to be called gridlock. In the seven sessions of Congress prior to Clinton (1979–1992), just over 600 laws were passed per session, 34 pertaining specifically to finance. With the Republican-controlled Congresses of the Clinton years, the number of laws passed fell precipitously (to 293 in the 1999–2000) session. During the eight years Clinton was in office, an average 94 finance laws were passed per session, an increase in the proportion of all legislation from 5 percent to 25 percent.[19] Because the surplus came in the context of diminished entitlement and fiscal discipline, absent was the public sense that it could be a resource that might address greater societal ills or indemnify the present against future downturns through public investment. Rather, future uncertainties could be met by further reducing debts so that these would not become a burden when times turned tougher.

While monetary policy achieved a prominence that earlier monetarists could only have dreamed of, the Clinton era also upended what had been the monetarists' strongest conceptual suit against Keynesian tenets. Milton Friedman, dean of neoliberal economists, was president of the American Economic Association in 1967. That year, he addressed his constituents with the news that government attempts to lower unemployment below a "natural rate" (the NAIRU or "nonaccelerating inflation rate of unemployment") were futile and inflationary, upending decades of convention in which it was thought inflation and unemployment could be traded off (a previously observed relationship graphed as the Philips curve). Others, like Nobel laureate Robert Lucas, drew the same conclusion about the limits to government intervention by noting that businesses would expect boosts in demand and raise prices accordingly (these responses were dubbed "rational expectations"). Finally, a man who would become Clinton's own Treasury secretary on his way to Harvard's presidency, Lawrence Summers, argued that taxes themselves were an impediment to investment.

Interestingly, the 1990s saw the Treasury Department converted into a central arm of foreign policy in an attempt to get the rest of the world to accept U.S. models of domestic austerity and monetary policy. Alan Greenspan accepted the grail of the NAIRU, and as unemployment continued to plummet in the late 1990s, he took every opportunity to warn against inflation as job rolls swelled. The expected inflationary effects of unemployment never materialized. The relative weakness of trade unions to deliver higher wages and increased productivity extracted from workers suggested that anti-inflationary obsessions had more to do with labor discipline than with concern over costs to consumers. By the end of 2000, unemployment had fallen way below the supposed natural rate of 6 percent, down to 3.9 percent. Global multinationals like Lucent and DaimlerChrysler were adroit in their announcements of large layoffs that largely affected overseas workers or in reporting reduced workforces when their domestic subsidiaries were sold. Such firms managed to signal both to labor and to investors their tough disciplinary stance in anticipating inflation without actually losing their skilled workforce.[20]

A different state of nature was required to justify persistent obsessions with inflation. If labor's interest in sharing the wealth was, by definition, inflationary, and if inflation was the paramount ill for a healthy economy, what could be said when even rising wages did not produce the expected inflationary effects? The resulting rhetoric would be called the "new economy," a term sometimes used to suggest that the good times would continue forever because the economy was immune to recession or, more modestly, that high productivity could accompany low inflation and unemployment. Wages might have been starting to rise slightly for those who saw the least of them, but in more general terms, people were living as if they had more money than they actually did. In effect, the American people were giving themselves a raise by spending more than they made. A visible aspect of this trend was the expansion of consumer credit through the issuance of credit cards, which in the United States approached a trillion dollars in purchases ($2 trillion globally, so that the United States accounted for nearly half the credit card market). Between the late 1970s and late 1990s, the average of monthly income charged increased from 3.4 percent to 20 percent.[21]

Another way to expand income immediately is to borrow against assets like a home, or against the promise of future income like stocks. On the former, homeowners' share of the value of their homes has fallen below 50 percent (it was nearly 80 percent in the 1950s).[22] Economists would rationalize the later by saying that people are spending their future dividend income today on the expectation that the value of their stocks will continue to rise. Similarly, banks would give out more than the present value of a home on the assumption that its value will appreciate over the course of the mortgage. In 1995 banks introduced high-loan-to-value (HLTV) second mortgages that allowed up to 125 percent of the current market valuation to be lent, with the understanding that banks can dispossess borrowers of their homes.

With deregulation of banking, abetted by the Depository Institutions Deregulation and Monetary Control Act of 1980 (which repealed mandated fixed interest rates for savings and loans), more kinds of financial institutions were getting into the act. In 1980, fewer than 1 percent of all financial institutions offered home equity lines of credit. By the end of that decade, 80 percent of banks and 65 percent of savings and loans did. The market had grown from $1 billion to $132 billion. During the same period more than a thousand banks were closed or merged with others.[23] The availability of mortgages was once a sign of prudent savings rather than consumption. Home ownership itself was a major factor in mitigating strain from inflation as value would appreciate to preserve levels of equity.[24]

In contrast, the present tendency toward leveraging ownership against future increases in valuation generates increased vulnerability to bankruptcy. If bankruptcy were declared, the home continued to bear the costs of principal, interest, taxes, and insurance. What was once a source of security is now a source of risk. Between 1979 and 1997 personal bankruptcy increased 400 percent, with a disproportionate concentration among baby boomers, a stunning collapse in the midst of prosperity for those managing middle-class lifestyles with low incomes—a self-designation invoked by three-quarters of Americans. Bankrupt homeowners carry nearly identical overall debt burdens compared with those who avoid it, but nearly twice the burden of short-term debt that carries the immediate demand to pay. For the one in ten households that experienced bankruptcy during the 1990s, the future could not be kept at bay and came crashing into the present.[25] The elimination of savings that these increased consumer debt loads suggest is akin to the post-Fordist just-in-time production that reduces inventory but also means that we live in a perpetual present without a buffer for the future.

By some measures, Americans have subsequently become more adept at managing increasing debt loads after the crash courses in consumer credit and debt of the 1980s and 1990s. During the 1990s, the number of households owing debt payments that exceeded 40 percent of their income crept upward. Yet, by the end of that decade, and in contrast with prior trends, there was no reported rise in credit card delinquency or bankruptcy.[26] This self-assigned raise must embrace a measure of risk, and this increased risk is really what is mandated by the new economy. In the 2001 annual report of Clinton's Council of Economic Advisers, the experts say as much, "Indeed the rewards of the New Economy are associated with risk, since the economy depends more heavily than before on financial markets, which remain volatile."[27]

The policy implication of this dependence on financial markets is noninflationary growth, an orientation secured by Greenspan's continued tenure at the Fed after Clinton left office. This is a disposition to growth without the exuberance considered by Greenspan to be "irrational," whether with reference to the stock market or the economy in general.[28] It would seem that even recession, if short in duration, was a reasonable instrument to wield to curb excess. Growth rates over 4 percent that characterized the last years of the millennium were seen as a problem to be tackled, rather than a benefit to be celebrated and shared. Too much success was a source of anxiety for those who would govern the new dependency. Reflecting on the career of growth in the U.S. economy, Robert M. Collins shows a change in its basic value as a social good that transcends any specific variation in growth rates:

> The pursuit of growth has evolved into an essentially technocratic endeavor, still central but now more circumscribed than before. Growth remains an important societal goal, but is, for the historical moment, conceived of in a longer time frame (therefore the emphasis on sustainability), evaluated according to lower expectations, and harnessed more closely than before to the need for price stability and a measure of fiscal probity.[29]

Whither Progress?

The newly declared dependence on financial markets pronounced so matter-of-factly by the president's 2001 economic report has been the source of great controversy. What started in the 1980s as a concern over the decline of the middle class and erosion of the American dream became, as measured prosperity took hold in the mid-1990s, a debate over the costs of success.[30] The stronger claim that emerged is that the economy is not simply dependent on the finance sector, but modeled upon it. As one sympathetic observer put it:

> We are seeing the *financialization* of the American economy. This awkward word describes a profound change, perhaps as momentous as the acceptance in the 1930s of government intervention in the economy. Historically, activities on the

financial markets—the buying and selling of stocks, bonds, and other financial instruments—have been regarded as far different from the day-to-day endeavors in the real world. People worked for years at jobs, and businesses built up expertise producing real things such as cars and shirts; meanwhile, financial investors merely traded pieces of paper in pursuit of high returns.

This distinction is quickly disappearing, as the high-risk society becomes as fluid and as competitive as the financial markets. Boundaries and barriers that once restricted and contained competition are being dissolved in the interests of boosting growth. . . . The combination of high uncertainty and unrestricted competition is reducing the difference between the real economy of factories and offices on the one hand, and the financial markets on the other. The rules governing Wall Street now apply to the entire economy.

The implication: In the high-risk society, workers, businesses, and countries must start thinking like investors in the financial markets, where the only way to consistently achieve success is to accept risk.[31]

To ameliorate the volatility that comes with risk, income averaging, layoff insurance, and stock-market-like income markets are proposed. Notice that in this reckoning financialization has as much to do with treating all economic activity in the same way as it does on seeing an equivalence between individual workers, businesses, and governments: all become agents subject to the same structures of opportunity and decision. These interchangeable entities share four characteristics: "(1) uncertainty of rewards, (2) ease of entry, (3) widespread availability of information, and (4) rapid reaction to profit opportunities."[32] This is not a list that will offer much surprise to captains of industry, for whom they will seem simply to be rules for doing business. But if the term *consumer* replaced *worker* as a means to put that ugliness behind one's more general consciousness of life, *financialization* aims to make life like an approach to business, and thereby return the protocols of work to daily life with a vengeance.

Here, risk will replace labor as something taken rather than given, as a venture rather than an appropriation of one's effort. Labor is still disavowed even as it is extended to the home and hours away from the job. Negative effects are not the return on unwanted bosses, but something one accepts as a consequence of seeking prosperity. Yet achieving wealth is also blended with the necessities of survival, since the older protections have already been removed and we have no choice but to embrace the new economy.

Other accounts of the new economy are more exuberant still. Commonly in these accounts, a rather utopian gloss on the economic and experiential implications of the Internet is expanded to embrace this new way of life. A typical example is Stan Davis and Christopher Meyer's book *Blur*. These business consultants tend to make their case through individual examples they deem "best practices" that then stand as generalizable trends. Davis and Meyer see increasing connectivity, speed, and intangibility of value based on information and relationships as the wave of the future. It is as if life were to become an ever-accelerating e-mail exchange. To be caught up in this vortex is to be unable to see the world as anything other than a blur whizzing by. More prosaically, *blur* refers to an undermining of social divisions and, with these, distinctions in how one identifies oneself. The direct connections between people make regulation unnecessary, and the complete sharing of information will mitigate price volatility and render financial risk obsolete. With the only value-generating source being what one has to offer, supply and demand disappear as discrete and opposed sides of a market relationship to be replaced by an ongoing process of exchange. As capital and labor become one, unions are a thing of the past, as is corporate loyalty.

The blurred self is securitized, one who offers shares in future earnings to investors. So while working for a firm, one is always also seeking money-making opportunities outside it. The new lines of conflict emerge when entrepreneurial activities that firms encourage their employees to undertake on behalf of the company's profits are turned to the worker's own accumulation of wealth. *"Take up your company's challenge to be entrepreneurial, whether or not your boss makes it easy for you, but insist that you be a real capitalist, not just a psychologically oriented one."* Implied is a Hobbesian war of all against all as capitalists do battle over whose self-interest is to prevail.

A hypercompetitive world such as this requires constant attention to opportunity and vigilance as to potential threats. There is nowhere to hide, and no moment of respite from the exertions of financial activity. "Managers check their voice mail while the pasta is cooking and compose e-mail while the baby naps. Even Sybil couldn't switch personalities that fast. *For better or for worse, in the blurred world, the 'work you' and the 'home you' have to meld."*[33] The reference to schizophrenia is not pursued. Nor is the downside to such madness. But as a feature of the world, *blur* acts as both noun and verb, naming a condition and prescribing action. It is not something that one can have a judgment about. There are only varying degrees of success in attending to these demands.

The loss of a haven is taken up more critically by many commentators on the foibles of financialization. George Ritzer, a sociologist who has written extensively on the cultural effects of commercialization and consumption, has worried that the implosion of monies earned in the past, present, and future—but all spent in the present—constitutes a market-driven manipulation of time that increases expenditure at the expense of mounting disorientation. Another sociologist, Robert Wuthnow, who writes on the moral dimension of the economy, recently suggested that the privatization of money, its status as a taboo topic of conversation around the dinner table, has led to an inability for parents to pass on to their children the ability to make financial decisions. Money becomes an isolating subjective force that makes people feel radically alone, with no institutional redress. "In consequence, capitalism functions less as a taskmaster, forcing us to do something we would rather not, and more as an alluring siren, compelling us with stories of its wonders and irresistible charms."[34] His concern is that the American Dream no longer organizes the contradiction between job stress and job satisfaction. Without a clear orientation to the future, discretionary income is frittered away, spent without planning.

That this book is based on research done in the early 1990s may be among its most instructive aspects. Within the course of a very few years, the separation between public and private financial spheres, upon which his arguments depend, seems to have been significantly eroded. If money was, even in the recent past, what people were thought to be more defensive about than any other subject, the veil has, in many ways, been lifted.[35] If a family watches television together, they will be seeing no end of invitations to discuss their financial future and to think about each other as imbricated in decisions taken today on behalf of tomorrow. The furious proliferation of money talk in the media permeates the home to a degree difficult to imagine only a few years ago.

The clear delineation of public and private, objective and subjective domains regarding money, has a powerful intellectual pedigree extending back to Georg Simmel's 1900

Philosophy of Money. "Money, by and large, is most influential in those parts of our life whose style is determined by the preponderance of objective over subjective culture."[36] It follows that if the objective increasingly figures in creating the sense of self, then the attempt to isolate those parts of life determined by money from those whose style is free of finance will become an untenable endeavor.

Curiously, one conviction that has run through the work of commentators of various ideological stripes is that prosperity has generated expectations that cannot be met but that people feel compelled to pursue to the detriment of their life satisfaction. Robert Frank has argued that the proliferation of high-end goods raises the frame for what counts as the norm, leading to what he calls "loss avoidance." He notes that even as real income has risen dramatically over time, measures of satisfaction have remained constant.[37] Luxuries lose their *lux;* the aura of the Lexus is profaned. Robert E. Lane reports that amid the relative constancy of satisfaction people feel with their material progress, there is a "spirit of unhappiness." This amounts to a decline in those since World War II willing to report themselves happy, an increase in depression, greater distrust of institutions, and a fall in the belief in progress, all of which he attributes to a famine of warm family relations.[38]

Others have announced Americans to be "spoiled rotten" and recommend a healthy dose of evidence to show that life really is better in order to overcome the sense of "anxiety and social decay." For example, purchasing power parity, the main means used to establish equivalents across space and time, overadjusts for inflation; GDP is undercounted because of excluded household production and increased value of leisure time. Further, between 1970 and 1995, when real wages declined, total compensation, including defined-contribution pension plans and health insurance, actually increased.[39] Moralizing accusation and tough-guy invocation aside, the difficulty in establishing the continuity of measures of happiness, satisfaction, and progress cast doubt on the transhistorical ways in which these terms are asked to function as comparative points of reference for daily experience.

That intergenerational improvements in standards of living do not translate into a positive state of mind should invite some rethinking of what it means to experience economic change. One of the defenses of prosperity in the United States notes that there is "no objective measure of happiness" and admits, "We don't know whether economic progress brings happiness, but we strongly suspect that the absence of it yields misery."[40] Cox and Alm, the authors, go on to argue that the "poor are not getting poorer," because their levels of consumption are rising, even if their incomes fall. The larger issue becomes how to translate point-for-point comparisons of individual commodities to the larger construct of what counts as economic life within a given social context. For this, the discrete and reductive measures, whether undertaken by triumphalists or naysayers, will remain a problem for assessments of how people situate themselves amid market dynamics. The consumer goods touted as measures of improved living standards do not advertise how they are actually made use of so as to engender a sense of well-being or improvement. Their immiserating absence operates more in the present by way of unsustainable comparison than as a departure from what was known in the past.

Another invocation of a future lost to diminished faith in progress is Richard T. Gill's *Posterity Lost*, which notes that the process of immediate, ongoing improvement undermines the idea of progress to be realized over the long term. By disposing and posing problems, progress as practice presents the future as empirically and morally indeterminate, an agnosticism that promotes present-mindedness, a shortening of time horizons that Gill terms "temporal myopia." The financial link is a psychological state that leads to a cycle of increased debt, decreased savings, increased gambling, and teenage sex—a state of affairs that can be broken by recognizing that it is not "logically necessary."[41] The family is the arena in which to reclaim faith that would in turn consolidate economic rationality and moral self-discipline.

From a quarter more sympathetic to market strains and the need to ameliorate economic pressures through economic means, Juliet Schor has authored some influential books that portray Americans locked in a cycle of overwork in order to sustain patterns of overconsumption. Schor arrives at her assessment of overwork empirically by adding estimates of moonlighting on and off the books to standard measures of per capita national income. She estimates that, between 1968 and 1987, an extra month's work was added to the amount of time the average worker clocks in a year.[42] She follows this study with another that argues that diverging incomes among those who pattern themselves after the same models or reference groups generate a rise in consumer aspirations that are unsustainable, resulting in anxiety, frustration, and dissatisfaction.[43]

If people can overreach in their susceptibility to influence by advertisers keen on selling more, Schor reasons, they can also reverse this trend toward escalating work and consumption by volunteering to lead simpler lives. This she calls "downshifting," an exit from the fast track to less expensive lifestyles, more simple tastes, and more time for humane interactions. This refusal to accept the logic of blur, this effort to reject the speed-up of life, could be seen as an opening salvo against financialization's unnerving effects. While some economists have supported her calls to action, she has also been taken to task by those politically sympathetic to her who have questioned the viability of a voluntary reduction of needs that would result in freeing time. To these concerns she has responded, "My work emphasizes the importance of *time* in reproducing human relationships, and the trade-offs between free time and earning money."[44]

Schor and others have popularized the notion that time is scarce and choices need to be made to free more of it for use outside the markets for labor and consumption. Yet the idea that less time is available for voluntary pursuits has been directly challenged in work by John Robinson and his collaborators. Robinson claims to be as uneasy as Schor is about rising "materialism," and as interested in finding "ways to slow things down," but wants to place the blame with "culture" not "capitalism."[45] Robinson's substantive critique of Schor is that she overestimates how much people work and underestimates how much leisure is available to them. His approach promises a truer measure of time use, namely, time diaries filled out by individuals for every fifteen minutes in a twenty-four-hour period. His research documents a tendency among respondents toward overestimating how much they work and how little they play. The diaries unearth fifteen-minute time nuggets in abundance (which amounts to a gain of an hour of free time per day between 1965 and 1995). They also document that much of the nonworking time is funneled into television watching (now 40 percent of "free time").[46] Progress is reported regarding gender equalization in domestic work, in productivity (if people work less than they report), and in time available to those at the lower rungs of the income distribution. The time spent with children and sleeping has remained constant.

This sunny picture, at odds with reported dissatisfactions and dim perceptions, is meant to suggest that far more can be done with what is available to us than is presently taken advantage of. While Robinson also focuses on the upper strata in the wage distribution, it is to make the opposite point to Schor's—that the more people work, the more they engage in other forms of voluntary activity, civic participation, sports, the arts, and other self-actualizing kinds of activity. The simplified message is that work is redemptive and that television erodes character. Hence, there is an opposition between economy and culture. But the more complicating aspect of this work is the relation between time-based satisfactions and the culture of its measurement. The successful completion of the time diaries implicates the respondents in a broader phenomenon of autosurveillance, constantly checking oneself out to see how things are going. The diary does not create time management; it only reports how well assimilated such acts of measurement have become. Although Robinson wants to give a progressive taint to this process, called "time-deepening," the infusion of the home with such thorough modes of accounting becomes prima facie evidence that freeing time from more general economic logics may be harder than could be imagined.

Time, in this account, remains a natural object, albeit one that can be compressed or expanded.[47] The fifteen-minute units of the time diaries are said to assume a zero-sum quality where doing more of one thing entails doing less of another. Time is unidimensional, linear, and physical. "Our time-diary records can therefore be seen as something akin to the physical artifacts, such as bones and tools, available to archeologists."[48] Above all, time is discrete. Fifteen minutes may be an arbitrary duration, but it inscribes a division between different kinds of human activity: contracted time (working and commuting), committed time (housework, child care, shopping), personal time (sleeping, eating, grooming), and free time (media intake, socializing, education, etc.).

But for free time to be free, it must be independent of the other categories. If someone is using a home computer to answer e-mail from work or a work computer to check investments, talking on the cell phone to the boss while food shopping, or coordinating the evening's meal while at work, these temporal domains are no longer discrete but also no longer singular in aspect. It may be that all these domains promote multiple activities, or thinking about one thing while doing another, or multitasking, which render units of time indeterminate and measurement improbable if not impossible.[49]

In this regard, financialization does not simply blur boundaries so as to create seepage; it insinuates an orientation toward accounting and risk management into all domains of life. This statement does not mean that all times and places are the same, but that, precisely in the spirit of the time diaries, they are all subject to the same culture of measurement. Time diaries are less artifacts of time use as a physical reality than of time measurement as a cultural imperative. The diaries themselves reference an ability to subject oneself to a mode of account and the embrace of the indeterminacy that follows when the culture of measurement fails to contain and control the thing it seeks to manage. The apparent precision of the study only serves to highlight the discrepancy with the more general confusion over what to make of time, once one is directed to persistently make something of it. The confusion of sign and referent, of measure and thing, has, understandably, led to frustration among researchers that the general population does not share their optimism about the future. "People are doing better than they think they are, but their perceptions of what is happening are increasingly flawed. It may be difficult to find or appreciate, but *there is time for life.*"[50]

The proof of the statement lies in the very study that even busy people undertake, but that ironically only exacerbates the flaw. The discrepancy between perception and reality, between mounting affluence and stagnant satisfaction, is the consequence of this compulsory self-rationalization tendered in the name of time for life. It is the recognition of wealth's effects, the efforts to grasp them through measurement that generates the disorientation, not some imagined deficit in the ability to mount a healthy appreciation of the facts of life's improvements. Time diaries purport to disaggregate what polls seek to aggregate, and in that regard they explain the discrepancy between time lost and time multiplied.

Poll data from the end of the decade continue to report increases in number of hours worked per household, declines in leisure time, and inflation in the annual income level considered affluent (up 50 percent in five years to $155,000). This trend is accompanied by an upward drift in the proportion of those who believe the American Dream to be more attainable than at the beginning of the decade. Yet even these fairly straightforward descriptive statistics reveal disparities between preferences—for example, for more money rather than more time *and* for a low-paying job they love over a higher-paying one they hate. If time were returned, as Schor and Robinson request, its principal allocation would be for more sleep, followed by hobbies, reading, exercising, doing nothing, watching TV, and making love.[51]

With sleep in the lead, it seems that the American Dream has been literalized, a desire for more time to expand the collective unconscious rather than more time for expenditure. Another poll, this one confined to Internet users, found a majority who agreed that "help getting things done would greatly reduce the stress in my life" and, by the same percentage, respondents who would like to use the Internet as a personal assistant.[52]

In the New Economy's Embrace

Whereas time diaries are applied by researchers only over a single twenty-four-hour period, the logic of self-monitoring and autoaccounting disbursed at fifteen-minute intervals reaches its apotheosis in the travails of day trading, the quintessential conflation of financialized work and home where time is both suspended and accelerated to a withering pace. Day trading entails the active buying and selling of stocks directly through a home computer. In its purest form, all trades are to be completed within the same day so as to avoid the consequences of losing money overnight, as the market reopens to unforetold volatility. For professional fund managers trading in other's money, the overwhelming majority fail to "beat the market" by doing better than a broadly indexed average of stocks (estimates of those who succeed vary between 10 and 20 percent). In other words, relatively few professionals manage investments better than the unmanaged fluctuations of the market itself. One hundred years ago, a visit to a physician had a 50–50 chance of benefiting the patient's health. In any other profession, brokers' success rates would be considered a scandal. When such success is achieved, therefore, it is highly prized and highly concentrated, with 63 people making the investment decisions for $6 trillion in mutual funds. Day traders, while of varied backgrounds, are equally rare in their ability to best the market—between 70 and 95 percent of them lose money.[53]

Technically speaking, day trading came into existence with the 1990s stock market expansion as a function of the confluence between home access to live data on stock price fluctuations and lowered costs per trade. But day trading became the poster child for financialization of daily life, the idea that an average person could transcend institutions and occupations and make money simply by managing one's own financial decisions. Stop working for someone else, work from home, and get rich quick in an electronic gold rush. Joey Anuff and Gary Wolf have written a spirited insider's account of day trading that is shaped as a time diary. It is a frenzied day, repeatable until the money runs out, in which each moment is unique and each day is the same. The vigilance of the time diary is endlessly repeated. Such repetition is numbing and dumbing, hence their book's title *Dumb Money*.

Day trading is lived as an interior monologue with the self, hence the authors' invocation of first-person singular narrative to explain the lure of their trade. "Thousands of unremarkable people have already become ultrarich. Last year I finally woke up to the Big Question. Why not me?"[54] The ordinariness of the newly wealthy helps to temper the rarity of achieving wealth. Here, money seemingly comes from nowhere, from the depths of quotidian experience itself, from activity neither work nor play, but in a reinvented domestic space suspended between intervals of interrupted sleep. This new self-concept and sheer communion with money for nothing is the only cost of admission, and it requires the embrace of a different ethos. "If you want to experience the glories of the new stock market, even vicariously, you need to have its main rule inscribed not just in your brain but in your stone-cold heart. Here is the rule: You are not an owner. You are not an investor. You are not an employee, customer, or stakeholder. You are not a patriotic American waving the flag, glad to go long in the name of freedom. *You are only in it for the money.*"[55]

Day trading seems to vacate the self of all human attachments. It eludes roles, old or new, stable or blurred. The pulse is set to the modulations of the market, and then only to stocks that show dramatic movements in price that can be joined before they change direction. All else is distraction. Attention is frazzled in wanton anticipation. Predawn consciousness (the first entry is 4:50 A.M.) comes when an automatic timer turns on the TV. "'How long has the TV been on? Have I missed the open? Did I oversleep?' And it takes all the effort in the world to turn my head and look for a quote from the red numbers on my digital clock. It says 4:50:06. The TV has been on for six seconds. I have won my first victory over the numbers. Attentiveness builds slowly from there. Lying in bed, I notice a sensation that is halfway between Christmas morning and the day of your first sphincterotomy, a creeping sensation not of alertness but of anticipation and anxiety. I couldn't go back to dreamland if I wanted to."[56]

The dream seems vitiated by the means deployed to attain it. The apparent solipsism of the immediate conquest of numbers must confront its opposite—the day trader is not alone, but spends the day apart but very much together with others making and breaking each others' fortunes. This incessant awareness of others who complete the self is organized through competition but expressed as regret. "Regret is the day trader's most intensely felt emotion. It is the key to his or her personality. . . . I've been around lots of traders, and I know that the only thing they like better than bragging about their profits is mourning the profits they didn't make."[57] This snapshot is the counterpart to the first, an equally hyperactive sociality. An incessant comparison of success lost that nonetheless depends on others in a kind of ongoing confessional. The day trader needs to sell but also to tell. Solidarity is found in mutual loss, the momentary possession through others of what could have been. This is a different sort of speculative mode that betrays desires other than money for its own sake.

Whatever privacy there may be to staying at home is less about putting others out of mind than about removing oneself from their scrutiny of the foibles of the market. The day trader has a reticence to be seen when constantly falling short of others' expectations:

> Maybe some people enjoy sitting on a wobbly chair in a musty room full of traders, but the last thing I need is the three-hundred-pound hotshot at the terminal next to me convulsing in ripples of giggles as I sputter curses at my disobedient momentum plays. Trading always involves the risk of losing; and losing, at least in this era, in this country, always has something furtive and shameful about it. Eventually you wrap up the shame in a 'funny' story. But at the moment the whip comes down, I want my door to be closed.[58]

Privacy comes less in the security of being safely at home, which is, after all, what generates these conditions of risk, but in response to necessary exposure. What began as an avoidance of all ethics seems to bring an ethical pressure to bear in the form of a hypersensitivity to loss in the eyes of others. Financialization engenders this selfless self-consciousness. To appreciate Anuff and Wolf's account of living the bull market at home, it should be compared to the statement of one of the profession's anointed heroes, a "wizard of Wall Street," market beater Frederick Reynolds of Reynolds Funds, as to what he sees and what he wants the world to look like. "Ideally I want the economy growing at 2 to 3 percent. I want inflation and interest rates to be low. I want the Federal Reserve to be fighting inflation. Everything has been really nice the last few years."[59] No dizziness, no shame, no subjectivity. Just nice. When monetarism becomes you, there is a world that lies waiting.

Between the anxious day trader and the placid fund manager lie the lived fibers of finance's web. Those who make rather than are made by the market are few and far between.[60] The gold rush of the 1990s bull market has passed, and with it has likely gone the greatest bulk of day traders. As the phenomenon has been flushed downstream, much rubble is left behind. The picture provided of the day trader is one of apparent anomie and amorality that is caught up in the disciplining forces of the market. Ordinariness trumps moral superiority that accompanies so many narratives of the rich. The day trader is offered as a character whose ordinariness also admits of a will to excess, a type for whom there are no secrets, only the avoidance of shame for failed efforts.

However fleeting day trading may be as a cultural phenomenon, it was the most visible advertisement for the home computer as moneymaking device. Such advertisement is necessary given that (by one reckoning done in 2001) less than 40 percent of Internet users in the United States avail themselves of on-line financial services of any kind—banking, professional guidance, or freewheeling trade.[61] In 1998, there were an estimated 3 million on-line investment accounts, with this number expected to increase fivefold in four years.[62] The following year (1999) Securities and Exchange Commissioner Arthur Levitt estimated that in five years (since 1994) business had grown from nothing to more than 7 million Americans who traded on-line, accounting for a fourth of the volume of all trades made by individual investors.[63] Levitt, until 2001 head of the nation's regulatory entity for the stock market, felt that nothing had altered the basic framework for governing trades. Levitt did think, however, that many trading on-line are gambling not investing, and therefore most will lose money, putting the legitimacy of the markets at risk. Levitt was clearly making a pitch for the professionals on behalf of the industry. When the speculative bubble burst on technology stocks in March 2000, so-called "active traders" (those who trade two dozen times per year) that Levitt had in mind did cut back on their activity, but the "hard-core" day traders (said to number in the tens of thousands), who buy and sell dozens of times in a day, actually increased their intensity in the subsequent bear market.[64] This observation is another way of saying that it took more work to make the money.

A very different picture of the moral disposition of wealth is presented in a popular account of the ordinariness of those who make money, *The Millionaire Next Door: The Surprising Secrets of America's Wealthy*, by Thomas J. Stanley and William D. Danko. Whereas Anuff and Wolf amalgamate their voices into a single figure of a day trader, Stanley and Danko create a no less singular image of wealth through their 500 personal interviews and 11,000 survey respondents accumulated over twenty years of research. Four years after its publication in 1996, 2 million copies of the book had been sold, roughly half the number of millionaire households it reports to exist in the United States. By the authors' calculation there should be 5 million more readers for the book. It is aimed at those who earn over $100,000 per year (recall that this was the figure for what was considered wealthy in 1996) but who do not accumulate wealth. The austere and unsung heroes who serve as models for the un-thrifty constitute the American Dream returned, now as the ability to become rich in one's lifetime by dint of hard work:

> The millionaires we discuss in this book are financially inde-pendent. They could maintain their current lifestyle for years and years without earning even one month's pay. The large majority of these millionaires are not the descendents of the Rockefellers or Vanderbilts. More than 80 percent are ordinary people who have accumulated their wealth in one generation. They did it slowly, steadily, without signing a multi-million-dollar contract with the Yankees, without winning the lottery, without becoming the next Mick Jagger. Windfalls make great headlines, but such occurrences are rare.[65]

Against the images of conspicuous consumption, indebt-edness, excess, and disheveled domesticity that mark wealth publicly, Stanley and Danko offer a portrait of "prodigious accumulators of wealth." This silent majority of the wealthy in this country obey seven cardinal rules that start with liv-ing "well below their means." Also on the list are efficient allocation of time and resources, financial independence valued over status, financial independence from both their parents and their children, fidelity to long-term invest-ments, and singularity in their occupational choice, most typically as owners of small business.[66] The villains of their tale are the "under accumulators of wealth," those who have the money to be rich but who eschew frugality for lux-ury. They could but they won't.

The populist turn in the book is that the usual predictors of wealth, family background and education, are not fetters on opportunity. A mobile home dealer or plumber who drinks Budweiser can trump an attorney or cardiologist who needs to wear a Rolex for credibility. Stanley and Danko go to great pains to show that their sample of millionaires scrimp and save, drive plebeian automobiles, and act like social Darwinists toward their children. Their life is devoted to building a nest egg that would make them dependent on no one, hence the definition of wealth in terms of net worth rather than income.

This austere figure of the millionaire effectively reinvents the ideal of the middle class as the petite bourgeoisie, for instead of focusing on home ownership as key to security, these millionaires concentrate on ownership of property as a small business and nonspeculative stock portfolio. They do not constitute a group with significant control over social wealth, those whose decisions affect the broader contours of how wealth is amassed, but rather delineate the financial threshold at which one has control over oneself. Those who own their own businesses are free from bosses and from risks of layoffs that come from being an employee. Stanley and Danko offer this example from an "entrepreneur": "What is risk? Having one source of income. Employees are at risk. . . . They have a single source of income. What about the entrepreneur who sells janitorial services to your employers? He has hundreds and hundreds of customers . . . hundreds and hundreds of sources of income."[67]

The authors caution that businesses do present risks but hasten to add that facing risk builds character. Risks are undertaken not for the thrill of speculation, of winning, but to improve moral fiber. It is tempting to ask, "What is all this deferred gratification for?" Personally very little is offered by way of life vision or ethos beyond a reassertion of the rugged individual beholden to no one. Ideologically, the authors' insistence is that being self-made, without family or government assistance, is still possible in America. What is intriguing in this account is how much, after all the frugality, it winds up looking like the day trader's mantra, "You're only in it for the money." Money guarantees freedom, but freedom has little substance beyond the assurance that one has accumulated money. The circle is complete if not as vicious as the one portrayed for day traders, but then, this is not an account of how people make their money but of what they do with it.

Both these books could be considered symptomatic of the boom. By the beginning of 2001, attitudes toward economic fortunes, measures of pessimism, were returning to what they had been during the last recession at the beginning of the 1990s. The difference was that the economy, by measures available at the time, was not yet in a recession; there was merely a decline in rates of growth. The sensitivity to change in trends was most noticeable in terms of general concerns about inflation. Hence, while 56 percent of Americans thought the economy was likely to get worse, 70 percent were worried about inflation and rising prices.[68] The primacy of the concern with inflation, over and above concern with the economy itself, seems to be one enduring legacy of the boom. Whether the future is perceived as dim or bright, whether the present hopeful or bleak, the knowledge that inflation remains the keystone to control of prospects endures. No matter how fickle the polls, how much they fluctuate, it is the sensitivity and legibility of their signs that remain.

Financialization helps account for the nonexpansive expansion. True, for most of the 1990s little trickled from the well-oiled wealth-making machinery. By the time, late in the day, that modest redistribution kicked in, the boom was declared dead—a contraction seemingly made to order by inflation's nervous Nellies. A trickle, not a flood. A hissing leak without a blowout. Economic indicators wax and wane, but fear of inflation remains the same. A rhyme fit for the nursery and the pensioner's home. Accumulation posts every success but the reference of what it is for. Inequality is unjust, and redistribution of wealth is a needed palliative. But when wealth fails to spell prosperity, something is rotten. And not just in the state of Denmark.

2 When Finance Becomes You

When does financialization begin? Many offer advice. Just as the good Dr. Spock taught the science of child rearing, so today households must be instructed on the proper approach to making kids financially literate. When scientific management was brought into the home, financial matters were a parental affair. Children would be protected from the market's madness, and money was to be kept off the dinner table. Secreted from money's corrupting influence, the home could be a haven, and children could live in blissful innocence of their full dependence until, with adulthood, they were shown the door. For the avatars of youthful finance, such insularity is morally irresponsible. After all, childhood as an interval of economic chastity is a historical and cultural aberration whose days may have been numbered with the fate of the west in the twentieth century.

Not that financialization harkens a return to the child labor of early industrialism. No, the clock would need many more backward turns to the agrarian family as economic engine and the Greek household as *oikos*, the basis of production. Properly taught, money management for children is not only a preparation for future employment, but also a means of rationalizing the home, of modeling domesticity along the lines of the modern corporation. And at present, the corporation is an agent of both industry and finance. So too with the self. Henceforward, child rearing will marry the discipline of hard work with a managerial approach.

A multitude of organizations have sprung up to promote this historical shift. BernieBucks.Com is one among many that offer educational products for "children's personal finance," namely, a book and software CD-ROM with graphics for Bernie's Super Cool Savings Plan (for only $19.95, plus $4.95 shipping and handling). The product features eager Bernie beaver building up savings. Children can issue their own checks. On a web site fortified with one testimonial from a woman in Tempe, Arizona, BernieBucks makes a series of promises. "Be prepare [*sic*] for complete involvement with your children as the valuable lessons Bernie teaches transfer from the pages to the hearts of your children. See them grow and experience the self-confidence that financial security can provide. By blessing your children with the gift of financial knowledge you arm them with the gift of financial power." In this case, complete involvement entails plunking the child in front of a computer to use that gift from Grandma to "form a relationship with a bank and learn how to monitor his money through the computer." No more winsome indolence or complaints of boredom. "With renewed vigor your children will awake to begin a productive day of earning money and watching it grow."

Other entities, like Cash University founded by Willard Stawski II, "create educational products designed to teach children about money." Their mascot is Cashew the squirrel, like BernieBucks, a cartoon mammal with imputed financial qualities. Stawski, a former stockbroker, now turns a profit as an "activist in financial education, working with chartered schools, banks, and credit unions." This activism to promote charter schools as captive markets for a financial curriculum stands as a surer bet than plying stocks. Such privatized education initiatives introduce thinly veiled singly tracked vocationalism into early grades. Stawski's advice is collected in *Kids, Parents & Money: Teaching Personal Finance from Piggy Bank to Prom*.[1] At first, it seems his suggestions are entirely generic, unrelated to the matter at hand: "Take time to talk with your kids and let them know how important they are to you. Once you've established a basic level of communication and trust, they'll be receptive to anything you say." Perhaps this injunction most resembles the rampant antidrug campaigns which assume that addiction emerges in the yawning gap between parents and children as a substitute for love. Parents must breach self-censorship and broach taboo topics. Talk to your kids about money (or drugs). No more secrets. Let them know you care but offer the tough love of a dangerous world. Familial financial bonds appear to be modeled on this kind of tough love. As BernieBucks says, speak truth to power and the danger disappears. Similarly, Stawski wants to "protect family members" from personal financial illiteracy (9). His method, like all sturdy scientific knowledge, is empirical, the result of "parental trial and error" (xiii). Although they were objects of experimentation, he doesn't think his own kids are too messed up as a result.

Tellingly, his own children figure in one episode of the book. Tragically, they are unreceptive to the modes of parental communication offered them. They are playing with a heap of toys procured on demand from the parents who found it easier to purchase the inexpensive items than to argue the merits of each individual object. Stawski discovers the kids destroying the little goo-gahs and attempts to get his children to pick up the toys but to no avail. His drill sergeant persona fails to get notice, as does his "I'm-about-to-kill-you voice." He begins to discard the toys himself and gets glee-ful participation from his youngest child. "I was losing it. I couldn't believe what was happening. My kids actually did not care about their toys. All of those items that were so im-portant in the checkout aisle were now meaningless to them" (74). So much for commodity fetishism. Not only were the kids unwilling to allow these products to become their means of life; they didn't even care for them as objects. He is appalled at his children's indifference to what he be-lieved they had hitherto prized. They were turning their backs on the world of value and therefore on his values. He realizes the deeper issue, "an overabundance of possessions with no pride of ownership" (73). Epiphany. His system is born. "We needed to develop a system that would enable our children to experience what adults in the real world do. Instead of taking the easy road and giving our children what they want, we needed to have them pick an item and set a goal. If our children are influenced to defer gratification and actually earn the dollars necessary to obtain the goal, they will experience the pride of ownership necessary to appre-ciate and take care of the goal item" (74).

At the time, Stawski had a successful brokerage firm and was able to free his children from want. His discovery is that the American Dream of abundance should not be inhabited by children, but should remain a dream deferred. The no-tion of deferred gratification had emerged in the 1960s to ex-plain why poor kids couldn't get ahead. The inability to save kept poor kids poor. A little more will power. Better impulse control. It was their call. Stawski was applying the culture-of-poverty argument to the vaunted middle class. Value of ownership comes when the desire to possess is resisted. Ab-sence makes for longing, and children would need to be de-nied if they were to become truly acquisitive. But it would seem that the deferral of gratification also spelled the end of childhood as the realm of freedom it was once imagined to be. No longer absorbed in the present, children would now undertake "to experience what adults in the real world do." The delightful indifference to property that set childhood apart would trade its pleasures for "pride of ownership." A parent's uncontrollable rage at having his authority impugned could now be turned to the moral high ground of goal attainment. Though the father did not act on his impulse to "kill" his children, he did devise a "financial intelligence plan" to terminate their childhood. In this respect, the family home takes on the trappings of the modern state, rational governance underwritten by threat of force.

For the family to operate on a rational basis, rules must be made explicit, and all information regarding how the household is run needs to be transparent and available. But financially literate families are not only rational; they are successful. Like businesses, they have targets or goals that they must meet or exceed. This purpose is achieved through the promulgation of a family mission statement. "The family mission statement is what can keep a family on course. If everyone is clear on the direction in which the family is moving, there will be little question as to which course of action to choose. Once this commitment is in place, it can eliminate doubt, create stability, and give every member of the family team a sense of belonging, meaning, and direction" (29). Of course, the notion of being a member of a team came to business through sport. The practice of total quality management imagined the kinds of intimacy and commitment engendered by family life. This management ideal is here being reexported to the family, carrying with it the expectations of business productivity. Presumably the good of the corporation and the individual are to be harmonized.

Stawski offers a series of questions that can be used in formulating the mission statement: "What is important to you as a member of this family? What can you do to help the family as a whole? What do you think your greatest strengths are? What are some weaknesses you may need to work on? What can other family members do to help you? What do you think our family goal should be?" (29). As a means of securing maximum participation for maximum output, the management-team approach assumes equality even if, unmentioned and at the end of the day, father still knows best and gets to be the "leader" of the family.

Like the tale of disregarded toys, the rationalization of the family along the lines of a business plan offers more a solution to the irrationalities that must be kept in check than a promise of wealth or happiness. Happiness is the absence of disorder, and wealth is the absence of debt. By paying off outstanding debt, "you can free yourself from financial bondage and experience the rush of personal liberation. Once you experience this freedom, you'll never return to financial rudderlessness and your children will be financially literate enough to never have to experience the malady for themselves" (10). Bondage and freedom refer to dependency on parents, who, in failing to teach "destiny control at an early age," may never see their kids leave the nest. This approach is supply-side economics with a vengeance. Self-discipline and not salary scales or rent control determine whether a young person can be financially independent. If the family is no different than a bank, debt can be morally deleterious.

As with team-based approaches to management, the confidence (or gamble) is that the underlings can be empowered without compromising the advantages of the leader. The delicacy of achieving this shift in domestic economy is more remarkable when one considers what is being suggested by way of full financial disclosure to the children. Under the familial ancien régime, secrecy was power. Children were made, not born, by denying them access to the cash nexus of the marketplace and the inner workings of the homeplace. Stawski's system consists of a series of forms through which all manner of income, debt, and credit are to be enumerated. What would keep literate children from demanding full disclosure? Goals and expectations are to be laid out on what is called a "com-tract," in effect a juridical model of family communication. Demands and responsibilities are to be written out and evaluated. In one worksheet, parents keep track of time when children begin and end tasks, and get to rate children's task performance as so-so (75 percent), good (100 percent), or excellent (125 percent). Children learn the pleasures of measurement under this new math that establishes the norm of the curve at 100 percent. Whether this is grade inflation or escalating demand remains to be determined. And what if children want to turn the tables? What governs the extent of transparency?

Family journals are to be implemented as a "public record" with separate entries for private matters. And what would police the distinction? Public entries adumbrate "positive attributes you are proud of in that team member" (64). Negativity is banished to the private realm. "Be sure to mention that the journal isn't an outlet for negative feelings that may develop between family members. Negative feelings are usually only temporary, and the journal represents a permanent record" (64–65). Assuming the kids do move out, the journal is a measure of family success. "The family journal is like your retirement fund, but instead of saving dollars, you are saving memories" (65). Can one retire on sheer positivity? The accumulation of memory is grounded on an active forgetting of whatever might dissent from the steady march of success. While Stawski's book begins with an account of toys, it ends with advice on how to get kids hooked up with stocks, bonds, and mutual funds. The developmental logic and behavioral protocols are meant to assure that as fully vested individuals, children connect the dots that lead to literate financial self-management.

The question of public and private domains within the transparent family refers not only to what one discloses and what remains hidden, to responsibilities shared and powers reserved, but also to two kinds of economy that are to be managed within the household, one for services in kind, the other for money. The distinction is in evidence in advice given on how to administer an allowance for children:

> Do you believe your kids have a certain amount of responsibility around the house just because they are members of the family? If so, those responsibilities have nothing to do with allowances. In fact, if those responsibilities are not fulfilled, the loss of privileges would probably be more appropriate than the loss of allowances.
>
> How can a child manage their money if they don't know how much they will be getting on a regular basis? On the other hand, if a child does not need their allowance that week, is it acceptable not to do the chores? And finally, do we want your children to ask "How much?" every time you ask them to do something around the house?[2]

Despite the penetration of financial markets into the household, the labor of running the home should remain unpaid. Chores are an obligation to family life. An allowance should be allocated based on a predetermined list of what children should be expected to pay for to teach the principles of money management. It should be calculated based upon what parents already pay out per week in incidentals for the children. When these little calculations are aggregated they come to quite a chunk. In 1995, teens 13 to 17 years old were estimated to spend $89 billion, $34 billion from allowances.[3] Five years later the estimate was $200 billion with another $250 billion in influenced purchases.[4] Kids can negotiate for a raise, but parents should never withdraw funds as punishment.

The allowance is for learning, not a reward for good behavior. The lesson should be that the cash nexus is noncoercive. From *Inner Self Magazine* we learn that children are "natural sales people." These abilities are often lost to adolescent peer pressure. When money is securely theirs, artificially inseminated by parents, they can assume their natural roles in sales. "Let them know that all income comes from selling, and that mastering the sales process is the most important skill they can gain to aid in their financial independence."[5] Allowance, then, is to be conceived of as capital, as expandable and not simply expendable income. This conception, too is a natural trait of children, as we can learn in *Atlantic Monthly*'s "Turning Childish Greed into Grownup Capitalism." "Children are instinctive capitalists. If you give them enough leeway, they quickly become shrewd managers of their own finances. When parents fail in their efforts at fiscal education, it's usually because for reasons of their own they have managed to make saving seem punitive and dull. Money is fun, and it's almost entirely self-explanatory."[6]

The separation of the fun world of money and the ethical responsibility to the household preempts constant haggling over what needs to be done around the house. Parents should avoid a situation where children ask "how much?" every time they are asked to clean their room. Without an allowance, the kid is cast as "salesperson and manipulator" and parents "do all the work." The difficulty lies in how to teach management without reference to labor. If money is attached to work performed, then the parent is seen as an employer. As employers have learned, too much emphasis on individual exchange between labor and output can turn attention to the shortfalls in compensation. The standard managerial dilemma would be how to increase productivity without paying too dearly for incentive. Layoffs, downsizing, reengineering are standard to the repertoire. Can you fire the kids when they underperform? The trick is to get the abstraction of time rather than the immediacy of the parent's presence to take on the bad cop inducements of the economized home.

Many university extension programs have undertaken to teach "financial socialization." Consider the following list from the University of Missouri:

> Try guiding and advising rather than directing and dictating how your child should use his or her money.
> Encourage and praise the child rather than criticizing mistakes or their actions.
> In fact, allow children to make financial mistakes. There is as much learning from a mistake as from success.
> Be consistent while taking children's differences into account. The individual personalities your children have will show up in how they choose to handle their money.
> Try including all family members in money management discussions and financial decision making as is appropriate for their age.
> Finally, explain to children what they can and cannot do with their own money and the consequences of violating the limits.[7]

Let time do the squeezing, and you won't have to. The children can then do it to themselves. The market runs with its

invisible hand, and so can parenting, unless limits are violated.

If money and the market can become the harsh taskmas-
ters, then parents fly free. Mom and dad can provide the
warm haven from the world they have foisted upon their
kids. With domestic labor out of the picture, money can become a topic of communication whose balm resolves all
conflict. At another public university's proprietary site, the
University of Minnesota Extension's "Children and Money
Series" takes a developmental approach to early financialization. Children and parents should talk about their feelings, values, attitudes, and beliefs about money. The kids
will understand that compromise over money conflict is
necessary. Every transaction is a learning opportunity. This
learning can begin "when children can talk in sentences."[8]
And so it is that concepts of earning, spending, and saving
comprise the terrible twos. A little math is required before
children can grasp borrowing and savings. If chores are nonnegotiable, where is the time to come from for all this learning and earning? "The time devoted to earning money
should be taken from children's leisure time, not from time
used to study or perform household chores." Time applied
to the unpaid domestic economy is inviolable. Time for
money is negotiable and expandable, so long as the proper
trade-offs can be made.

Play does not disappear, but it is structured around moneymaking activities. No idling in the imagination. Play
"bank" or "grocery store"—wholesome activities that promote counting—not "doctor" or "house," which may lead to
more carnal attentions. Development assumes that children
overcome problems posed by a particular stage. Preschool-
ers "cannot differentiate between reality (a commercial) and

fantasy (a TV program)" (7). This inability provides parents the opportunity to discuss actual products advertised in the commercials, identified as a "suggested teaching activity." Reality belongs not only to what can be held in the hand, but also to what can be bought and sold. If the kid can own it, it must be real. By early elementary grades, children should be pocketing the change they earn clipping coupons, contributing money to "religious and other groups of your choice," and seeing the bills for everything bought for them (8). Earning in earnest can begin in elementary school with a paper route or "extra tasks" that parents find them (9). They should be budgeting, shopping, saving, cost sharing. By early teens, business start-ups, inclusion in family financial planning as to how to cut expenses, and comparison of rates at different banks are all on the agenda. With middle teens, parents should dump their children from the allowance dole, get them to help with tax preparation, teach them how to deal with risk of financial loss, and be sure they allocate time for study in light of work demands. With all of this guidance, children will be chomping at the bit to jump ship.

Thus far, all the advice has been directed at parents to impart to their kids. Parental authority aims to engender independence. It also oversees a dual economy within the household. The allowance permits engagement with the market, while the private sphere of the household remains unpaid. Parents are entitled to punish aberrations in this private domain, but the public is one over which their authority is limited. The domestic economy is run on a transparent accounting system that patterns consumption for children. Investment is the next frontier to delineate the new dual economy of the household. Minimum age requirements for stock or mutual fund ownership vary from state to state between eighteen and twenty-two, although custodial accounts can be opened for younger folk, (and exceeded 2 million according to a recent Merrill Lynch estimate).[9]

Teen investment advice is framed more as a recruitment tool for those who want to pursue a career in the markets, but the literature itself is directed at the pleasures of teen moneymaking. "Investing is good for you, but it can also be endlessly fascinating. 'I do this because it's fun,' says Dan Abrahamson, a Connecticut high school student. 'When I was ten years old, my big passions were baseball cards and comic books. My grandfather convinced me that I should buy stock in Marvel Comics. I bought it at 20, and it went to 56, split two for one, and then I sold it at 31. It tripled in about a year's time. I was hooked. I started watching CNBC. My grandfather and I would call each other with tips. We'd talk every day'" (8). The personal connections of grandfather merge with the innocent games of trade. Nothing is abstract here; use and exchange are lined up directly. Pleasure moves on, however, from possession to ownership. Suddenly the expansion of price is more fun than the fading memories on those scattered tokens of authenticity.

Familial bonds are better formed around the financial news than on old pastimes. But financially interested teenagers should have nothing of this nostalgia for items passed from hand to hand. Touch now rests with the keyboard, and teenagers have come of age economically before they can even consider political enfranchisement. "Online trading has made it possible to buy and sell stocks less expensively and more easily than ever before. So more and more people see the stock market as a normal part of their daily concerns. This book will explain the ways you can get involved in trading—and making money—now, even before you're old enough to vote" (2). Clearly, the transit between television and computer screen is most intimate and immediate in financially literate households. The attention to advertisements suggested in the developmental schema mentioned earlier needs to be refined in light of the profusion of spots for financial services. This media attention is the reality that parents should be discussing and involving their children in. "When it comes to making money by investing, time is on your side. Start early. You probably know something about the stock market. If you watch the news on television, you can't miss the daily reports of what happened on Wall Street. You may have seen business magazines around the house, or your parents may talk about stocks at the dinner table."

The buzz is all around, and children are perfectly primed to partake because they have been encouraged to make mistakes. Making a mistake with money means losing it. The willingness to lose in the short term for the prospect of long-term gain is definitive of financialized childhood; after all, the younger you are, the more risk you can afford because you have the chance to make up for your losses. However, conquering the trepidations of being risk averse that can creep in during those teen years should be rewarded accordingly. The book from which all this sagacity is drawn is called *Streetwise*. While the reference is to that little byway in lower Manhattan, the title also alludes to the rough-and-tumble ways youth learn from the territory they take over as gangs.

Monied teens are encouraged to form gangs of their own, called investment clubs. These clubs are cauldrons for the budding democracy of the street, laced with a smattering of social Darwinism. In one example, "'Students get to vote according to their share of ownership.' That means that seniors, who have been contributing to the portfolio for longer, have a greater share than new members. That way the kids with the most experience—and the most risk financially—get a larger voting share" (156). Since risk is a measure of reward, those with the most to gain have the greatest influence. Before teens can vote in official elections, they learn how power is exercised so as to render universal suffrage moot.

The financial services industry recognizes that the games children play can shape their future, and the industry wants to ready its employees before they are distracted by the academic pursuits of college. On offer are games, contests, and simulations from TheStreet.com, Fortune.com, Yahoo, E*Trade, Forbes, America Online, Salomon Smith Barney, MainXchange, Stock-Trak Portfolio Simulations, CNBC Student Stock Tournament, Investment Challenge, Virtual Stock Exchange. The securities industry has a trade association with an education arm, the Securities Industry Foundation for Economic Education (SIFEE), with its own entertainment, the Stock Market Game, launched in 1977. By 1999 more than 700,000 schoolchildren played the game in the United States alone (although prizes could only be collected by those over eighteen)—over seven times the number who participated a decade before (169). The games maximize risk taking because that's what it takes to win (as opposed to gain with actual investments). The games and simulations are also free of costs like taxes and of volatility like price fluctuations induced by buying and selling large volumes of shares.

The games also have a cathartic effect that can reinforce the norms of investment. A college student who began playing one of the games through an organization in high school provided a cautionary note. "I bought Amazon I think at

150, and it went to 90, and that's when the game ended. It definitely turned me away from ever wanting to day trade or time the market" (176). A finalist in another contest, Investment Challenge, admitted "Real-life investing is totally different. I would never trade options in real life. You can gain or lose 50 percent of your money in hours" (176). Such distinctions can be difficult to draw. Not only are the games portals to a future in finance, but they are sometimes linked to or fronts for commercial stock trading operations as well. Youthful exuberance can lead to furtive borrowing of a parent's credit card at the request of what appeared to be a game site. "Although it's fun to play stock market games via the Internet, watch out for web sites that take you, after a few clicks, to a real trading and investing function. It's easy to see how you might believe you're playing a game when you're actually entering stock trades" (180).

Games then can both invite an unrealistic appraisal of risks and beckon the player with unappraisable risk. Indeed, the Internet is a medium that does not recognize the distinction. What you see is what you get (WYSIWYG) pertains not only to the principles of software design, but also to the manifest plausibility of identity. Online investing aims to put the self-conscious teenager at ease. The Internet is a one-way mirror, not a looking glass; there are no judgmental peers; you are your screen name. No one knows you're a teenager on the Internet. Online you're just like anyone else. It's an ideal place for beginners, as you can ask questions without feeling intimidated. If you do feel a bit dumb, at least nobody knows you. If financial literacy is killing childhood, the Internet extends adolescence for a lifetime. The desire to watch without being seen, to engage in surveillance without judgment, will cover for the consequences of risks taken. Feel free to be ignorant. Any money you venture will be your own.

The cautionary notes are added to cushion the pain of potential financial loss. The cautionary symphonies, however, are reserved for those whose gains appear excessive. The former are meant to warn that succumbing to fear and greed—the foibles of human nature—can have tragic consequences. The latter may warn against the belief that the system itself is rigged. It is worth pausing, then, on the most notorious of teen investors, Jonathan Lebed. His crime was (as financial crimes are) in the eyes of his accusers, in this case the Securities and Exchange Commission, which investigated him for fraud and profiteering. Lebed at fifteen is distinguished as the youngest person to reach a settlement with the SEC. Lebed graduated from a stock market game hosted by CNBC in which he placed seventh, to the more lucrative pursuits of speculation in penny stocks or microcap stocks typically valued at several dollars.[10] These are companies with no registered profile that lend themselves to the kindness of strangers found in the Internet chat rooms. On September 20, 2000, after an investigation of his actions and interrogation of his person, the SEC put out a cease-and-desist order with the following allegation:

> In order to carry out the scheme, Lebed would acquire a position in a thinly traded microcap stock, buying between 17% and 46% of the volume on the day of his purchases. The momentum of this purchasing would often cause the price of the stock to rise. Shortly thereafter, almost always on the same day as the purchase, and after the close of the market, he would begin posting false and/or misleading messages touting the stock. Lebed used a fictitious author name for each message. For each stock manipulation he used multiple fictitious author names. Generally, Lebed would post 200 to 300 identical mes-

sages to various Yahoo! Finance message boards during this first round of postings. The next morning, before or as the markets were opening, he would send another wave of identical false and/or misleading messages (the same approximate number of messages), employing additional fictitious author names. On that day, as the stock price was rising in reaction to the hundreds of messages he had posted, Lebed would sell his entire position in the particular stock, always realizing a profit. The gross profits on the eleven transactions ranged from more than $11,000 to nearly $74,000.[11]

The account is given with all of the scientific precision of replicability. The SEC does make it seem as if any teenager could do what Lebed did (possessed of the same ethical failings, of course). And by Lebed's own account, everything he knows he learned on television or the Internet. He is one of the teens whose natural capitalist instincts were not crushed by his peers; just the contrary, they flocked to him. The story was given its greatest airing by Michael Lewis, first in a lengthy cover story in *The New York Times Magazine* (February 25, 2001) and subsequently in a book, *Next*.[12] Lewis at first can't detect the crime, given that all given names on the Internet are fictitious and naïveté rules the trading chat rooms. He also notes that Lebed gives up nearly $300,000 but gets to keep a larger, half-million-dollar slice of his earnings. This settlement resembles those bestowed on bigger fish Michael Milken and Ivan Boesky, who were prosecuted for billion-dollar frauds and allowed to keep the larger share of their gains. Lebed kept his cash without admission of guilt or acknowledgment of harm (no individual plaintiffs were identified in the case). Lewis speculates on the SEC motive:

> I finally came clean with a thought: the S.E.C. let Jonathan Lebed walk away with 500 grand in his pocket because it feared that if it didn't, it would wind up in court and it would lose. And if the law ever declared formally that Jonathan

Lebed didn't break it, the S.E.C. would be faced with an impossible situation: millions of small investors plugging their portfolios with abandon, becoming in essence professional financial analysts, generating embarrassing little explosions of unreality in every corner of the capital markets. No central authority could sustain the illusion that stock prices were somehow "real" or that the market wasn't, for most people, a site of not terribly productive leisure activity. The red dog would be off his leash. (59)

Lewis's piece came two weeks before the great bull market was declared moribund and after the gold rush of on-line trading dried like a summer streambed. The SEC's chief enforcer, Richard H. Walker, in response to being outed as a legitimation front for the stock market, countered by calling the analogy with standard brokerage practices of pumping and dumping "sophomoric."[13]

Ultimately, it is the regulator's own authority in assuring the integrity of the markets that is at stake. If a TV-watching teenager can do what pros do (for roughly the same compensation and often the same result), whither the industry? If truth and fiction cannot be separated in the investment arena, how to convince consumers that fairness rules? The Securities Industry Association, the ones who bring us the stock market game, are concerned enough about these issues to conduct polls on investor attitudes toward the profession. Even before the scandals that broke in Enron's wake, the two biggest reported problems (at 49 percent each) were "an industry motivated by greed" and "brokers or firms putting their interests ahead of investor's interests."[14] Like politicians, trust in one's own tends to be high, while faith in the aggregate is low. The survey has tracked an increase among investors in on-line use from 7 percent in 1996 to 20 percent in 2000 (7). On-line trading is considered by some 30 percent to be bad for the market in general, as it increases volatility (9). This response is understandable given that more than half of the polled investors engage in fewer than a half dozen trades per year (78).

Lebed is therefore a worthy villain, combining youth, lack of affect, moral indifference, hyperactivity, success—all the things that financialization of domestic life winds up promoting. His parents, however, are presented as the beneficiaries of his initiatives (he buys them a Mercedes SUV). They defend him, they curse the computer, they express their bewilderment at what has happened, but they are not his teachers and certainly not in control of his actions. Given this confused parental role, the state had to act as father. Enforcers stepped in and did what dads are not supposed to do—dock allowance. The respect for these great fathers fares no better. Securities cop Richard Walker is confident about the efficacy of his threats, "If I'm a kid and I'm pulled in by some scary government agency, I'd back off." Lebed does not seem equally impressed by their office. "I wasn't frightened by them because it was clear that they were focused on whether or not I was being paid to profile stocks when the fact is I was not. I was never told by them that I was doing something wrong and I was never told by them not to do something" (both quotes in Lewis, "Jonathan Lebed," 2001, 59). So he continued to pay attention to the authority that mattered most, and kept trading. The market has depersonalized the tangible power associated with moral instruction. The carefully crafted delineation within the household between public cash economy and private ethical obligation turns out to be as unsustainable as the moral boundary that sought to preserve the home as haven. When authorities are not well placed, appropriate means and ends become misaligned. The financialized teen is well prepared for the ambiguities that the present holds for the future.

Listening to the Market

Children can become financialized by accident or design. Older folk need to be sold on the idea. A thirty-second spot on television or a glossy magazine ad may tickle the passions but provide little practical knowledge. Since financialization is something that people must ultimately learn to do to themselves, primers are required. It is a burgeoning genre. Rather than being forgotten, the importance of books is preserved but made adjunct to the Internet. Just as live concerts and international tours promote sales in other media, books (albeit with sales in the millions) are portals to proprietary web sites. While teenager Jonathan Lebed was fined and scorned for taking matters into his own hands, for acting independently under the veil of custodial accounts, the tone of the primers is equally adverse to relying on financial custodians even as they act on this same authority in the name of dumbness or idiocy. On the other hand, the smart investor leaves all assets and deposits all risk in the hands of the professional adviser. The thresholds of time, resources, and expertise for doing sufficient research to make a fully informed decision on the intricacies of the market are too great to go it alone. Yet playing it smart can become less inviting as the large brokerage houses have become doubly suspect.

Here we see the salience of the problem posed by the relative paucity of professional fund managers who generate a higher rate of return than could be had by investing in a broad sampling of publicly traded stocks. For one thing, since few professionals can actually "beat the market," why bother with them (and, more to the point, their fees)? For another, if the brokers are in effect engaged in retail sales for the stocks their own parent investment banks have stakes in, who are they really working for anyway? These challenges on the basis of performance and of interest lead the do-it-yourselfer's march. If smart investors go with the professionals, then independence is for idiots, dummies, and fools. As in other linguistic contests over meaning, those denied legitimacy are designated morally deficient (who in their right mind would spurn expertise in such a technical field as finance?). Similarly, the abject wear the epithet of cognitive deficiency as a badge of honor. Or at least, this is *their* marketing strategy. It works for hip-hop sold to suburban white teens. It works as well for those entrepreneurs hawking do-it-yourself investment approaches. The reverse of the analogy also holds. Most rap artists never get the chance to cross over, as they are denied access to major distribution networks. Similarly, many self-help avatars only get to help themselves. At least the rappers get to keep the music.

The financialization literature fits well the pattern of other expressions of commercially inspired selfhood.[15] The highway between connoisseurship and pathology is multi-laned and well traveled. Idiots, dummies, and fools are the intrepid ones willing to speed along the high road of success. They must, however, be ever vigilant and increasingly absorbed. Success breeds excess. Pleasure unchecked consumes itself. The master of *Cook's Illustrated* magazine and of butter-slathered Julia Child may wind up crashing into the fat-balanced dietary science of *The Zone* or some equally disciplining tome. The tracts for gourmands and dieters lead to and mirror one another. The treatises on financial self-help welcome those with the hubris to make themselves rich and those with the humility to seek redemption for their addictions. When all the pages are turned, the many types merge into a great traffic mass. As the elements rely on one another, they should be examined one at a time. Fools first.

The Motley Fool, Inc., is, in its own words, "an Alexandria, Virginia–based multimedia company dedicated to empowering individuals to take control of their financial destinies."[16] What began in 1993 as a newsletter issued by brothers David and Tom Gardner became a web site hosted by America Online a year later and was launched as its own site in 1997. The brothers' nod to public service and the intense interest exhibited in promoting personal finance on public television were married in what amounted to a viewer-subsidized hour-long infomercial aired on PBS during 2001. Their written prose makes a modest claim: "This book will enable even the rankest novice to invest expertly on his or her own, enjoy the heck out of it, and *beat* market averages over long periods of time . . . all things that too many people think takes an expert, a Wise man, or a market insider to do—those Foolish enough, that is, to believe that the market can be beaten at all" (11). Sounds more like David and Goliath than David and Tom, and the pleasure that comes from slaying the powerful experts lends a moral high ground to the revenues they are able to generate for themselves.

Motley Fool is also an investment club whose membership is measured by the millions who have visited their site. The claim is that the powers of observation of these millions can outsmart the number-crunching intelligence of the pros. Iomega's Zip drives are given as an example. Some professionals doubted that the new firm could meet product demand before other companies soaked up market share. The Fool's visitors called their local retailers to find out where they would be on the waiting list for the data storage product. Another toured the manufacturing plant, and another checked to see how full the factory's parking lot was. All of this information was amassed on the site to provide a picture of the firm's capacity that justified further investment. Direct communication had triumphed: "We discovered some wonderful things (like how many people were willing to volunteer their own investment research for the benefit of many)" (18). With a booming market, the Fools boomed louder, beating the market in one year (1993) by 40 percent (19). Playing means winning. Otherwise a market index fund is the way to go. Beating the market, above all, means doing better than the experts, the professionals whose actions set stock prices.

Since the index is an average, a norm, beating the market is by definition a departure from conventional wisdom, which is what the Gardners mean by foolishness, the avoidance of "bad thinking." By increasing the volume and pace of information exposure, telecommunications drown out the good with the bad. "So, while modern technology has determined that we'll continue to pile up more and more information, technology has no good mechanism for ensuring that we even maintain our common sense" (21). Against the chaos and confusion of modern-day Babel is a call for a new ethical self. The unconventionally wise investor separates good information from bad and is in an informational environment, a model of human conduct. "Good investment practices can almost be called studies in good character. Warren Buffett's investment career, for instance, is not so much about balance-sheet analysis as about Buffet's own humility, patience, and diligence. Peter Lynch's approach is not so much about the price-to-earnings ratios as it is about perceptiveness, optimism, and self-effacing humor. The greatest investors are often outstanding human beings, insofar as they exemplify the highest achievement in one or more human characteristics like patience, diligence, perceptiveness, and common sense" (21–22). So they're not in it for the money, but for the virtue of the well-made decision. Monetary transactions can provoke the "baser instincts," and these must be combated at all cost, not the least because "fear and greed will ruin your investment returns" (22).

In order to make money you have to take some distance from it. This distance must be established both in space and in time. Distance in time allows for the embrace of risk. Professionals are paid to provide security and therefore promote risk-averse strategies. Fools play by different rules: "First is, invest money that you can afford to wait on. The stock market is risky. We like that very much; it helps us make money, because you almost *never* get something for nothing. But over a given period of time, your stocks could get mashed. . . . Invest money that you plan on keeping in the market for at least five years. (We recommend a lifetime). Second, invest in good companies. We buy stock in companies that dominate their industries, companies that have a sustainable advantage over their competition, companies featuring honest and efficient management" (27–28). Stock investments are a measure of life; let it be long. What one owns is a measure of one's own goodness, honesty, and efficiency. Ownership is a mode of self-possession.

The brothers Gardner profit from the advice they offer but present themselves as a different sort of expert. They're transparent; they practice what they preach; they're not divided between a wholesale and retail division. They use their own money and don't "front-run" by first investing in stocks and then recommending them to benefit from their self-fulfilling prophecies and advertised rates of return. They deduct commissions (and pay them as well) from their reported revenues. They reveal the hidden costs that come in the "bid/ask spread," the difference in price between selling and buying often pocketed by the middleman who matches orders. The brothers are owners who treat themselves as members of the club:

> Our aim at Fool HQ has always been to make our numbers duplicable by *anyone*. Everyone has to pay commissions and spreads—we do too—so we account for them. And hey, because we interact with our readers online every single day, we couldn't get away with anything less. Getting away with much less has been a commonplace for the past several decades of "one-way publishing," where publishers could impose their own standards and conventions—legitimate or otherwise—without fear of retribution. Welcome to the new millennium where your readership has now become its own community, able to communicate and organize itself with the ardor and coherence of a grassroots political party. Subterfuge just became that much more difficult. (269)

Never mind who has more capital to begin with. Information sharing and mutual assistance are the great leveler. If the high school investment club favored those with the most to lose, the Fools claim equitable treatment regardless of the size of the stake. These are familiar claims for Internet-based communications-as-community. The difference here is that material welfare is directly imbricated in this ethos of communication. This common interest is claimed as a primary identification and a basic instinct. It is precisely the sort of thing that nationalisms are made of: "Just as evolution taught the antelope to run in herds to survive the attack of a lioness, individual investors have been forming investment clubs around the country to help them keep a tight hold on their capital. Places like Fool.com offer that opportunity for collaboration, only now it's a twenty-four-hour operation and it's nationwide" (275). Whereas electoral politics may, like professional stockbrokers, have difficulty convincing people that the system works for the common good, the investment club offers flexible participation to suit any appetite. Against the losing propositions of winner-take-all competition, the club speaks the language of cooperation. When faith in professional disinterestedness has been eroded, the inner sanctum of expertise cannot hold its precious contents. Knowledge is freely distributed, and expertise is generated in the aggregate rather than being vested in individuals. What socialism is this running with the antelope herd? How did the authority of the lioness become so readily contestable? While Motley Fool is a parable of socialism, it is also an allegory of deregulation. Disintermediation, getting rid of all middlemen, is equated with disalienation, getting rid of elected representatives. The absence of proxies, whether brokers or politicians, leaves the market in its purest form, a collectivity of decision makers acting directly on maximum available information. Each person contributes a bit of information to the puzzle to create a picture of the whole from which all benefit. Because the whole is directly available to each of the parts, no mediation is required—other than that of the mode of information itself. And at $175 billion and growing by $50 million a week, investment clubs can rival the largest mutual funds.[17]

It would be just as easy to argue that these decisions are fully mediated, more so than any broker or politician could embody, but that approach would shift the weave to a different story. Motley Fool is a descendant of the SEC's 1975 repeal of fixed commissions that fostered the discount brokerage industry. A discounter, recall, is simply a company that is only involved in retailing stocks, not underwriting

them. Unlike a full-service investment bank that can afford
to lose money in stock trades to provide a market for the
stocks it has acquired, the discount broker only has volume
and volatility on which to generate its revenues. In the end,
however, the government looks after both kinds of company equally by sponsoring the insurance agency, the Securities Investment Protection Corporation, to fortify accounts against collapse (SIPC insures up to $100,000 in cash
and up to $400,000 in other assets). The do-it-yourself dis-
count house transfers labor costs to the individual investor,
who does the legwork for nothing. Motley Fool pools this
unpaid labor and packages it as a service from which the
good brothers benefit. They make no mention of profit sharing on their book, nor do they suggest redistributing the fees
they collect on trades. There are some corners into which the
lights of transparency and full disclosure do not reach.
When you sign up to become a Fool, all references are to the
service being free. Propriety rules do kick in. The Motley
Fool copyrights all information, although any individual can
use it personally. There are rules of conduct: no porn, no lying, no impersonating, no multiple identities, no viruses. It's
a clean machine. Then there is the disclaimer:

> You also agree that The Motley Fool will not be liable for any
> investment decision made or action taken by you or others
> based upon reliance on news, information, or any other mate-
> rial published by The Motley Fool. The Fool relies on various
> sources of information that we believe to be accurate and reli-
> able. However, we make no claims or representations as to the
> accuracy, completeness, or truth of any material contained on
> our site. There are literally thousands of contributors here,
> most, we believe, with incredibly interesting and insightful in-
> formation and opinions to share. But we can't and won't take
> responsibility for the accuracy, completeness, or even the truth
> of every post on our service. Remember: All information and

content provided on The Motley Fool is to be used on an "as is, with all faults, we're not perfect" basis.

Membership has its privileges but also its price. If you lose money through mutual assistance, you've no one to blame but yourself. This is a nation without a state, there's no safety net, no security blanket, and if you don't like it, you can leave at any time. All risks you assume will be your own, and that is all the fun of it. Motley Fool has its own public-private divide. The public domain is free discussion groups in which paid Motley Fool staff (designated with TMF tags on their screen names) answer questions. While all info is equal, the pros are more equal than many. There is much advertising for financial services on the site and easy ways to purchase these services. The site can be considered at first glance a kind of free distance-learning course, complete with tutorials and on-line help. Then there is the private room, the portfolio account where money changes hands.

There is nothing exceptional in financial self-help writers helping themselves to the revenue streams made available through ignorance. Few can boast the multimedia tie-ins of the Gardner brothers with such professed absence of self-interest. Ken Little had a bricks-and-mortar career at USAA Federal Savings Bank and was president of the San Antonio Economic Development Foundation. He now guides investor neophytes electronically for About.com. Little's contribution is *The Complete Idiot's Guide to Investing in Internet Stocks,* a universal self-help formula which assumes that lack of knowledge is no reflection on one's intelligence. The exotic world of Internet stocks is rendered familiar by packaging entrance to its mastery as no different than learning how to fix one's own pipes. But if a fool is a person skeptical of conventional wisdom, an idiot is one who can become inured to the anxieties of financial risk.

Risk can be calculated as a departure from expected gains that results from fluctuations in impersonal market forces; in coldly quantifiable terms, risk is "a measure of the possibility that an investment will not earn the anticipated return" (316). With Internet stocks there is only anticipation, as there is no track record of past performance to examine. Frontier metaphors abound, and the rush is on. Little promises to teach "how you can spot the gold among the fool's gold" (3). But for the idiot, risk is somatic and voluntary. Since moneymaking is an act of free will "You control the amount of risk you want to take. . . . You never have to take more risk than you can stand." Whereas fools are protected by running in a herd of their own, idiots need to be wary: "Watch where you step if you follow the herd—The 'herd' is more wrong than right." Like fools, idiots need to separate good emotions from bad. Greed and fear cloud judgment and dim reason. Pleasure is the true investment. "Having fun is the only acceptable emotion when investing in Internet stocks."[18]

The point of investing is to make money, and, fortunately for the already rich, "the more money you invest, the less time you will need and the less risk you will have to take" (50). For the rest of us, the means must justify the ends. Since investment is open to all regardless of whether they are rich or poor, the means test is affective not financial. It all comes down to your "personal risk tolerance," or "the level of risk you are willing to accept to achieve a goal" (49). "At this point, you need to do a little exercise in self-awareness. Spend some serious time considering your personal tolerance for risk . . ." (53). Risk tolerance seems to be at once something objective outside oneself that is freely chosen and a disposition hard-wired into the nervous system. Since price volatility can't tell you whether an investment decision is correct or not, personal anxiety must suffice. Little provides the following list of indicators for a bad investment decision:

> You can't sleep at night.
> You check the price every 15 minutes.
> You scour chat rooms looking for encouragement.
> You worry that when you are away from your computer that something bad is happening. (53–54)

Risk is a "friend" whose intimacy with your own emotional pulse allows you to know yourself: "Look at risk and your reaction to it as a barometer of your investing health. If you can make investments in Internet stocks and sleep well at night, then you are on course. On the other hand, if you toss and turn like a person in need of an exorcism, you probably have passed through your comfort zone and into that area between dusk and dark known as the starch-in-my-shorts zone" (57). Here is a Faust story for the ages. Risk is a devil to sleep with at night—a "voice" to listen to. Those who require the exorcism (of a professional broker, not a priest) will get ripped off, but they won't have to be bothered by it. The brokers won't let you at the real opportunities, which come from "flipping," or quickly selling stocks purchased as an initial public offering (IPO) at a much higher price when the stock is actually offered to the general public. "Institutional investors can get away with it, but if your broker let you buy shares of a hot IPO and you flip them right away, you may not see any more IPOs for a while. Brokers don't want you and other retail customers driving down the price by dumping stock on the market" (42). So while investment banks may underwrite or guarantee the initial price of a stock that they then sell in lots to customers of their choosing, risk is borne retail.

What keeps people from bailing on a system that seems so patently rigged? One factor is the ability to maintain confidence in the objectivity of the market, achieved by making regulatory mechanisms visible. The other is faith not in the vagaries of exchange but in the fundamental usefulness of what is being traded. Although the SEC is officially charged with combating stock fraud by, in part, determining who can disseminate what is meant to be self-prophetic information (and who, like Jonathan Lebed, cannot), the securities industry is hardly one to make much of its ongoing dependence on state intervention. The solution to this problem has been self-regulation.

There is nothing new to this self-policing. The National Association of Securities Dealers was created in 1938 by the Maloney Act as an amendment to the Securities Exchange Act of 1934. The NASD covers 680,000 industry professionals. A more recent development is that self-regulation, in distinction to its public twin, is to be a moneymaking venture in its own right. In 1996, NASD Regulation was made an independent subsidiary, and in the summer of 2000, NASD Dispute Resolution, Inc., became operational, with John Sexton, new president of New York University, as its chair. This fee-for-service entity accepted more than five thousand new cases for arbitration and closed an equal number in 2000 alone.[19] Privatization of conflict resolution does not displace the need for government regulation; it simply shifts the center of power to the Federal Reserve Board.

While corruption kills confidence quickly, over the long haul, the greatest threat to confidence in the stock market is inflation risk, which, when combined with taxes, can yield a negative return on investment. Little reminds us, "Under these conditions, you could quickly become discouraged and conclude that you are almost better off not investing the money at all. That kind of financial uncertainty doesn't bode well for the stock market" (52). In the end, government can't legitimate firms, but it is obliged to sustain confidence in markets.

Little's book was written before the spectacular crash of Internet stocks in March 2000 and the subsequent disinterest shown by venture capitalists to what had been so recently the apple of their eye. When investments soured, the new economy looked remarkably like the old one. Risk is an attribute of any investment, but the reason its embrace proved so crucial to Internet companies was that so few could show any profit. Given the newness of the phenomenon, the past could be no guide to future earnings. The present would have to suffice. Typically, investment decisions are run by the numbers, especially the ratio between the price of the stock and the annual earnings of the company (PE ratio). Since prices on new stocks can fluctuate significantly, the measure of the movement, or volatility, is also relevant. The difference between the volatility of an individual stock and the market as a whole is measured by the coefficient beta. Without a history of earnings and given the shenanigans of IPOs, supernumeration is hardly helpful and not always even available. If an Internet issue's peers are mostly IPOs, then no comparisons are available. "There is a real danger in hiding behind numbers to evaluate Internet stocks. The danger is that numbers work best when you can compare a stock to its peers and the market as a whole. The database I have built of Internet stocks is filled with more 'NA' entries than anything else, meaning that the numbers aren't there to evaluate" (83).

It's no wonder that insomnia and excess stomach acid become such important tools in risk evaluation. With the benefit of hindsight and collapse, the constructive meaning of idiot as willing nonprofessional slips into its pejorative twin. The metaphysics of the new economy rests not on the ephemeral quality of telecommunications (working the Internet is as tangible an activity as any other), but on the leap of faith entailed in investing in it, especially given the thorough quantification of the world.

A good bit of invention will be required to generate numbers by which Internet stocks might live, even if it remains unclear what is being measured. In Little's database of 253 pure Internet stocks, only 34 earn any kind of profits (118–119). Part of the mystery of the Internet has been how to make money on something given away for free. Like television, access is free to viewers and paid for by sponsors. Information service provider Yahoo! earned profits on advertising revenue from 1998 to 2000, but saw revenues decline in 2001. So what counts as a proxy for earnings that justifies investments? One factor is traffic, or how many people visit the site. Advertisers are charged on the basis of audience delivery, "unique visitors." Even with a sales-based site like Amazon.com, there's no ready way of translating, for example, the 14.5 million visitors in March 2000 into their sales accounts, which number 17 million. But for the purposes of charging advertisers, every "visitor counts as a sale" (129). Advertising becomes equally important for a new dot.com and is from this perspective not an unreasonable investment.

If an eye-catching prime-time ad can get people to visit a site, it's money in the bank, even if beforehand many will not know what the company "does." The address is the thing. More so than a Nike swoosh, a dot.com ad treats name recognition as revenue. While this was already a feature of advertising, namely, to associate the logo with a whole experience and not narrowly with a product, the dot.com ad provides an easy way to check out what all the noise is about without having to commit to any purchase. Like the producer relation in the Internet, the consumer access is free but revenue generating, in the sense that visitors translate into formulas for further market capitalization.

It's easy to see how Yahoo! could for a while make money, while Amazon (at least in its first six years of operation) could not. Yahoo!'s gains are much more fragile than Amazon's losses (for their seventh year, 2002, they actually projected a profit). One attempt to assess this difference is market viewer value (MVV), which divides the market capitalization, or total value of outstanding stocks, against the number of people who visit the site. High MVV means that you're paying a lot for that visitor, and perhaps the stock is overvalued. Yahoo! and Amazon were in the same ballpark here at $1,988 and $1,643 respectively (130). When you actually calculate sales per visitor, Amazon's were almost ten times what Yahoo!'s were ($120 versus $13) (131). Of course, Amazon has all kinds of costs in warehousing and shipping product that Yahoo! does not, hence the difference in profits. Interestingly, investors are paying for the promise of a public. The usefulness of the Internet, tautologically, is measured by its use. What is supposed to be a sales medium is more commonly approached, from the instrumental perspective of valuation, as an end in itself. It would seem that what is being quantified and profaned is the utopian promise of the Internet itself.

If the present turns out to be almost as uninformative as the past for Internet stocks, what about the future? "When you buy an Internet stock, you are basically buying a piece of the future" (83). From the perspective of investment, the future is not really different from the present but simply more of what we have now, or growth. Rate of revenue growth is a keen indicator of what the present looks like when read as the future. The problem, however, is that, almost by definition, rates of growth will decline as a company matures. The trick is to diversify sources of income (like stock portfolios themselves), such as merchandising agreements, referral fees, and other nonadvertising sources of income. If there are limits to such internal growth, then expansion through mergers becomes all the more important.

Betting on growth may prove too abstract a measure to get to the future. Alternatively, one can imagine what one likes in the present as the future. Little likes computer ads and so foresees customized ad streams as a way to crack the viewer sales problem. He also like networks: "Networks are the road to success. Being connected to a greater whole is more important than standing by yourself. Networks will manage your house and help you manage your life" (300). Whether or not this prediction is the truth of the future no one can say. But if numbers can't get you to take the plunge, desire will. Growing, well-managed companies are the bread and butter of long-term investment. They are good, but not necessarily fun enough to sustain interest. In this sense, professionals' advice (despite their antiprofessional rants) about investing in those things that please you is no different than Grandpa telling his little charge to buy stock in Marvel comics. Perhaps unwittingly, the question of what of the present we want the future to be gets posed through a mechanism we might have thought hostile to such valuative musings. The realization of want is what the utopian promise of the market is said to be. Curiously, Internet investment displays an interest in the profit-taking market to be something other than itself. If profits are not available, dreams will have to suffice. Staring close-range at a computer screen may be less romantic than promises of a world made one. Bleary-eyed intimacy is often the most practical consequence of collapsing time and space. For all that risk agitates locally within the body and monitoring personal finance keeps one in place, distance is forced on proximity, and the idea of the Internet has to carry where the actuality is quite mundane.

Throughout the financial self-help literature, reenchantment of a world profaned through attention to monetary reason is a persistent theme. If capitalism were hermetically self-rationalizing, the accumulation of wealth would be a self-justifying endeavor. Yet all of the how-to books add the caveat that money cannot buy happiness. Literacy, mastery, self-management are all intended to keep the disordering effects of living with money at bay. The authors ply their trade on the presumption that money is a problem that cannot fix itself. Wealth is the sticky problem bequeathed by a society that cannot offer the solution. That's where they come in. There is little novel in the categories of self-help. Most of the metaphors are adopted from other genres that assume a pathology from a demand (for beauty, sobriety, sanity) that cannot complete itself.

Financial planning professor Jerry Mason takes up the fitness metaphor in *Financial Fitness for Life: Advice from America's Top Financial Planning Program.*[20] The book is a paragon of planning, with checklists and quizzes with true-false answers provided. There is little room for ambiguity in these exercises. They are meant to be habit-forming. He labels "destructive beliefs" notions such as "People with money are happier than those without" and "You can solve almost any problem with money" (2). Financial fitness means knowing money's limits and therefore accepting one's own. To be fit means to accept one's place in a socioeconomic hierarchy, to not envy those with more or covet that which you cannot have. "Quality of life rarely correlates with the amount of money you have, but it does correlate with how well you manage your money" (5). Control is the key to a fit life. Mismanagement introduces "financial stresses" that strict adherence to the program can eliminate one by one (297). Fitness carves out a great middle like a Darwinian niche, where a harmonious relation to work, to debt, to charity, and to taxes allows the masses to live free of fear.

All this self-management requires ongoing learning and constant vigil to eliminate the flab of ignorance that will lead one to fall out of the fit middle class. Mason leaves the reader with confident clichés: "Knowledge will usually erase fear" and "Knowledge is power" (298). Applied reason for fervent decision makers, a steady diet of the right information will build a self-regulated body. In another paean to the powers of reason, organizations professor Max Bazerman offers a refrigerator metaphor of "unfreezing" and "refreezing" "decision patterns." "Money mistakes," like "overweighting momentary impulses" or "falling for vivid scares," reflect underlying psychological defects that, once identified, can be readily corrected.[21] For Mason and Bazerman, dumbness is no virtue (nor is irony) and being smart can trump the debilitating effects of too much affect.

Not all financial self-help invests in knowledge as the road to salvation. There are those who would rather climb a mountain than dally with Wall Street. They would rather chat in a coffeehouse than man a chat room. The vigilance required to exercise every financial muscle, to master every item of information, to manage each minute as if it were the one before, is an untenable burden. Knowledge may be power, but in finance it is a headache:

> In our journey through life, I think we can logically say that the more we learn, the better off we are. This observation fits neatly into the way we conduct our affairs, live our lives and survive in this world. Whether it is learning a new subject in

first grade, revamping a production line problem or becoming a better parent, the more we learn, the better off we are.

However, when it comes to investing, you can *kiss this logic goodbye*, because the less time you spend trying to learn everything there is to know about stocks, bonds and mutual funds, the better off you are. But you do need to know a few things, including how expenses and taxes affect your portfolio, and the lesson to learn is:

The less you pay in expenses and taxes, the better off you are.

There you go. Class dismissed.[22]

This is, no less than the others, an argument for a particular investment strategy, one that places faith in the long-run returns of the market (11 percent) and self-manages an indexed approach (some simulated diversification across the market as a whole). By eliminating the fees of a managed mutual fund over thirty years, the projected difference in what one has "saved" is more than $300,000 (121). This indexed approach means lowering expectations of retirement savings from $3 million to about half that and focusing on the "emotional complexity of saving" (136). "It seems to me that when it comes to building and maintaining our investment portfolios amidst the chaos that swirls around us, it's easy to bypass the inward responsibility of saving and focus instead on investment things that are out of our control, like daily stock market quotes, quarterly earnings reports and year-end mutual fund summaries, because looking at issues outside of us is a lot easier than dealing with issues inside of us, like our saving and spending habits" (136).

By leaving one's future to the invisible hand over which no amount of knowledge can yield control, we can focus on those matters that are inside us. Just when mastery seemed to slip out the door, it comes back in as self-control over what we want and what we can allow ourselves to have. This private domain is no less calibrated monetarily than the complexities of finance in the outer world. The assumption is that by reducing desires or redirecting them away from strict market-based calibrations of satisfaction, more time and space can be allocated for pursuits that do not touch upon financial management. Decolonization comes at the expense of any control over what may be colonizing the world in the first place, but, as is consistent in these tracts so steeped in rhetorics of change, politics as a means to change what is "outside of us" is rendered inconceivable.

Money at its most benign is a neutral and objective medium of exchange. Some New Age approaches to money see spirituality in the same terms. Jerrold Mundis, in *Making Peace with Money,* has a chapter on Enlightenment in which he adopts an ecumenical approach by now familiar to observers of the genres of financial advice: "Select a spiritual path that is appropriate for you."[23] Here too, making peace with money is not to be equated with making money, only with avoiding the travails of being subject to fiscal irrationalities. It is, in short, an attitude. "It means to create a relationship with money that is simple, comfortable, and free of stress, worry or pain; to create a relationship with money that is satisfying, even joyful. . . . You can no matter who you are" (1–2). This is not the joy that comes from betting right on a stock and beating the experts, but from not feeling like you've missed the boat when you're out of the game. The liberated self is one without unsecured debt. If you default on mortgage payments, that's okay; you can give the bank the house and walk away scot-free. If credit card payments run afoul of your means, the debt will chase you wherever you roam. Better to be homeless and free than to have creditors knocking at your door. The latter alternative may remind you that your spiritual health may depend on others. Interestingly, the temporality of Mundis's "peace" is not so different from the Internet space invader. The present's the thing.

To feel free of obligation and to reduce unsecured debt, one must repeat the following: "one day at a time," "tomorrow is irrelevant," "all that is real, ever, is today" (9). Mundis actually does acknowledge that the people to whom he is referring work to make money. Their mistake is to see misery in work as labor performed for the enrichment of another. "We experience work as misery mostly because we resist it or object to it. We will continue to experience it thus until we embrace its naturalness" (79). Part of the problem, however, with work that is wage labor is that somebody else can deprive you of it. Not to worry, you didn't need them anyway. "Remember: You're not unemployed, you are self-employed—in finding work for yourself" (334). Mundis even seems to have a solution for the problem of savings, given that this requires the discipline to defer a desire. "Saving is not money you are putting away, being prevented from spending, or that's being removed from you. Saving is spending. It is spending on investments. It is *buying* an investment. Even if all you do with the money is to put it into a passbook savings account, you are still *spending* it. You are spending it on *yourself*. But if that's true, what are you buying with it? Profit—the interest the bank will pay you back" (278). There's no problem with experts or high money-management fees here; since everything comes back to the self, nothing ever really leaves.

Other spiritualist treatments abound. George Kinder's *Seven Stages of Money Maturity: Understanding the Spirit and Value of Money in Your Life* compensates for those of us not brought up as financially literate children. Money has its own ontogenesis. We can begin as adults with the pain and innocence of childhood, progress to the knowledge, understanding, and vigor of adulthood, and then graduate to vision and aloha. The stages correspond to Buddhist chakras, but are readily transcribed into financial terms. Vision is the stage where "we see God everywhere. . . . Ted Turner's zeal to build CNN into a worldwide communications system is yet another example of Vision in action."[24] Aloha, handily "borrowed from native Hawaiians," signifies "generous and selfless blessing that transcend[s] the economic differences between us" (23). Nothing need be done to eliminate those differences, only to be respectful of those on either side of the divide (even if, in building an empire, the others you so admire are laid to waste).

An economy based upon exchange will assure that all receive something, for Kinder sees money as such as "the wine that brings out the divinity within ourselves and our community" (114). This conclusion he deduces from a sketch of money's social history: "Money widened the realm of giving and receiving; it fostered new relationships between individuals and added to the human capacity for freedom. With money, an infinity of gifts could be given and an infinity received. In a way, money was the original Internet. Money created a new, limitless world, one rooted in our sense of fairness and reciprocity with one another, a world similar to what we think of as paradise or the habitation of the divine" (114).

Within a few sentences we move from universal exchange to transcendent universality. Ontogeny does recapitulate phylogeny. The maturation of the self is simply following the evolutionary tracks of society. The result is to reinscribe the divide between public and private through a distinction and alignment of inner and outer resources even as the claim is made that "soul work" and "money work" are "woven together within the undivided space of our beings"

(127). Outer resources are salary and net worth. "Inner resources refer to those qualities of your being that contribute to or detract from your ability to achieve financial goals. The link between integrity, financial success, and Money Maturity makes inner resources as important as outer resources. . . . The issue is one of the heart not the head" (316). By this reckoning financialization is not the triumph of cold calculating reason, but an affair of the heart. It is a kind of embodied faith (an exotic, orientalized body at that) that will enchant the world of monetary exchange.

It is the presence of this other sensibility that brings money into line with security. This public-private delineation is entirely traditional—outer and inner correspond to paid and unpaid, visible and invisible, head and heart. On one hand, the ascription of this difference as one of Western reason and Eastern sublime, along with the gendered associations of thinking and feeling with masculine and feminine, neatly aligns race and gender with financial divisions. On the other hand, these dualities are to be sustained within each person, irrespective of the person's own social attributes in terms of race, gender, class.

The turn to the spiritual East to redeem the materialistic West is a common move in financial self-help.[25] It matters little that the East is decontextualized as a corrective to its heartless counterpart, and this Orientalist emphasis does nothing to shake faith in cold-war paeans to the evils of totalitarians left and right, South and East, First World and Third. On the contrary, "The history of Western capitalism demonstrates how dramatically creative a market economy can be" (182). The turn to the East also solves an ideological problem for a Christianity that taught separation between what belonged to God and what to Caesar or, more recently, a televangelism mocked for its holy rolling of the two into one. Given this collision course between secular and religious histories of the West, "we often find our 'God concept' must come in for a major overhaul."[26] If your God doesn't "do" money, it's time you rethought and let him into your finances.

This double embrace of God and Wallet promises financial freedom for those whose only guide was money itself. This imbalance constitutes an addiction, one that can take many forms, including "the compulsive spender," "the big deal chaser," "the poverty addict," and the "cash codependent." These are all variants of being "money drunk," for which Julia Cameron and Mark Bryan's twelve-step program is the cure. Freedom, it turns out, comes through constraint. Not only must you give up your will to a higher power, but you have only ninety days to do so. Because we're talking finance, time is money, and each step of the plan is rolled into a week. Sobriety returns with the recovery of clarity, dignity, authenticity, balance, accuracy, humility, trust, character, joy, self, compassion, peace. After twelve weeks, five days are tagged on at the end for "vision: the recovery of hope." Efficiency reigns here as well. It all begins with quantification: "*Counting* all of our expenditures will teach us a lot about ourselves" (119). By week ten, we've recovered the self by placing it on a time grid, a schedule in two-hour increments that, like the time-diary scheme discussed in the previous chapter, proves how much free time you possess. If there's something you want to do, just put it in. "What we *become* on the grid is consistent" (180). By week twelve we're ready to give up money-as-god for a money-friendly one.

The overhauled god turns out to be a shrewd money manager. Contact is not assured, a morning prayer is required along with a list of affirmations:

1. I allow God to establish my well-being.
2. I accept divine guidance in my worldly affairs.
3. I draw on divine goodness to fulfill my earthly plans.
4. My dreams come from God, who unfolds them through me.
5. I accept God's help in all money matters. (208)

Forget about tithing, the force is with you for the whole av-ocado. Addiction is quelled through routinization. There are affirmations for every problem.

No expertise is required to determine these problems, only the will to admit they are there. Addiction to money is determined through self-diagnosis. The external factor shows up "whenever money is a ruling principle that has become destructive to career, family, and a sense of self-respect" (16). And there the buck must stop. Were it to go further than the destructiveness of money it might prove too powerful a force for any god to handle, particularly if it were taken to be able to bring down civilizations, eliminate populations, propagate massive poverty or environmental decimation. Such dilemmas might take a bit more than ninety days to resolve, and who would possess the will to take on what does not singularly belong to them? Self-diagnosis, is not surprisingly, a "highly personal matter" (18), but as few as four of a list of twenty-two attributes can qualify people as money drunks. Among those attributes are: experience drastic mood changes because of money; argue or worry about money frequently; lie about their true financial status; avoid people to whom they are in debt; se-lect sexual partners on the basis of financial status; have a family history of money troubles; when speaking of money become sad or angry.

These criteria cast a pretty wide net. Poor and indebted qualify automatically. If you got rich by worrying about money and haven't stopped yet, you're in the pool as well.

Anyone in between who displays monetary affect is at least a bit tipsy. But if virtually anyone who dwells in the universe of money can be drunk, what does sobriety entail? Going cold turkey isn't an option, since being money drunk and money sober can entail fingering exactly the same amount of cash. Spending what you don't have to get what you want is close to money's symbolic function in exchange. The advent of the consumer credit economy is all about leveraging what you have to make more of it, and, with negative savings, this is what money has become. If credit money is now everybody's means of subsistence, then unburdening debt will have to suffice as a sign of sobriety—no margin calls, no hedge funds, no risk, just good clean use of what you have. And yet the overhauled God that suffers no negative emotion, that allows money to function properly, that allows one to accept one's place in the cosmos, to find equilibrium between what one has and what one can get, starts to sound a lot like the nineteenth-century liberal market.

Self-help is a kind of generalized advertisement for the market, a means of purging in the self what may be keeping oneself away from the economy's truth. In this regard, the literature on financial self-help resembles early advertisements from the 1920s that explained exactly what the problem was so that the product in question could present itself as a solution. Halitosis keeping you from getting ahead in life? Try Listerine. Drunk on money? Well here, drink this. Ironically, advertisements have moved away from this explicit narrative meant to justify acquisition of a particular item. Branding has meant acquiring an association with an experience that no pair of athletic shoes or soft drink could actually deliver. The ad itself substitutes for the product. The self-help genre is often not trying to get you to acquire something but to get rid of something (whether pounds or substance abuse). With finance, establishing lines of excess may not be nearly as subjective as Cameron and Bryan suggest. The consequences that kick in are largely in the eyes of the creditor—more so now that bankruptcy is more punitive thanks to recent legislative reform. The sense that you must embrace the pathology within, mine your inner life, and give yourself up to a higher power confounds the simple distinction between what is subjective and what is objective.

Financialization is ubiquitous, but never automatic. It always requires action that leads toward self-recognition. To subject oneself to the reason of finance is to assure that henceforward one will never act alone. The information gathered, the risks taken, the gains realized will be affected by what others have done, and this fact engenders awareness very different from what is presupposed in narrow self-interest. The financial self is never just one, never undivided, never simply rule taking or rule making. Reason can never be relinquished, but it is always disturbed. Just when it seemed we could be confident that reason was for quantifiable gain, it turns out that it is for life. How can we square these tensions of risk and reason that this fully financialized self augurs? The different meanings and usages of risk rarely see eye-to-eye. It may be time to bring them together.

3 Risking the World

Finance offers a word to the wise and foolish alike: Risk. Those averse to it should seek professional help. Those willing to cuddle in its embrace can power themselves. Those who have drunk too much at the well should seek a higher power. All this advice is available free of charge with fees collected later on. The suffusion of the world with risk appears unavoidable. While financial risk has the potential of loss, it is a recipe for reward. It is an ad for venture. But finance does not monopolize the meanings of risk, and that fact only makes the world a still riskier place. The uses of risk are many across the human arts and sciences, but the differences are not often recognized or reconciled for the demands they place on conceptions of selfhood.

Risk is the rage in sociology, the thematics of which have been trotted out in a series of books by Ulrich Beck and a few more by Anthony Giddens (and another in collaboration). The emphasis is on the uncertainties of ecological and technological developments, where the imbrication of nature and culture through an array of practices such as genetic engineering and nuclear power poses the threat of catastrophe beyond the threshold of any insurance. The ills of "manufactured uncertainties" like pollution confront people with the prospect of "collectively binding decision-making" that can engender a shared "burden" of responsibility to create a "risk community."[1] Ecological risk is an appealing basis of socialization for Beck because it constitutes for him a domain of interest and action that transcends national boundaries and is globally cosmopolitan. Further, revealing something seemingly in the province of nature to be socially engendered adds opportunity to danger. Conversely, the ecological presents itself with an ethical imperative that binds people together beyond a freewheeling construction of identity. Beyond the dictates of state and market, this notion of risk sociality is meant to open up a new domain of action not already circumscribed by dominant forms of national governance and capital. The reflexive society is one based on knowledge and the effects of "unawareness," or unintended consequences. Paradoxically, there is a temptation to admit the dangers of risk, acknowledge the limits to what one knows, and thereby remain unprepared for whatever unpredictable circumstances actually arise. The cycle of monitoring and uncertainty only multiplies dangers because when everything is full of risk, nothing cues people to take action. Risk awareness engenders a kind of complacency.

It is not clear how well these axioms apply to financial markets. If most investment professionals cannot "beat the market," more knowledge does not necessarily improve desired outcomes. Admitting that knowledge is insufficient might simply lead to avoiding investment, and therefore the reward of risk. At issue is the point at which information might actually resemble something like knowledge, as being action oriented in the manner that Beck describes. Stock market prices may rise or fall while information thresholds remain relatively constant. The market is treated as an ecology, as an environment obeying natural laws, and therefore welcoming to all who would come to discover it. Unlike natural disaster where exposure to danger is shared across the spectrum of participants, financial risk is a disbursement of reward that legitimates the dangers for those who are not the beneficiaries of events. Economists define risk as the measurable probability of an occurrence, whereas uncertainty is immeasurable. The distinction may be difficult to sustain conceptually, but the act of measurement and the consequences that follow from treating outcomes as the basis for prices can render such conceptual subtleties moot.[2]

The forecasts and predictions don't need to be right, but they do need to be quantifiable.[3] The case of Internet stocks illustrates this point well. There is no past upon which to forecast a future, but this lack did not impede measures of value from being drafted and applied to IPOs even if these turned out to be spectacularly wrong in many cases. The act of measuring itself performs the necessary service.[4] The same might be said for insurability. It is the application of actuarial calculation that yields a cost structure for premiums.[5] While financial risk beckons to all in the way that other manufactured uncertainties might, once the conditions of risk are accepted, the great sorting machine is activated. This is nowhere more apparent than in who gets bailed out when risks fail to yield reward.

Risk, in this regard, is a rhetoric of the future that is really about the present; it is a means of price setting on the promise that a future is attainable. Nowhere is this fact more evident than in futures trading, where, one researcher observes, "not only does the use value of money facilitate the circulation of commodities, but the future of each enters into the present instantaneously and relentlessly. How the future and present interpenetrate is what futures trading is all about."[6] Once the assertion is made that future and present interpenetrate, we are no longer talking about events that have yet to take place or life that awaits living, and it is difficult to know what separates the two moments.

For sociologist Niklas Luhmann, it is risk itself that "turns the page" between past and future, serving as the "irreducible residue" in what otherwise would be a present without time.[7] Risk presents not only the limit to what can be known in the present, but also the burden of acting as if one could know. If modernity is a compulsive movement of presents, risk helps explain how the past is relinquished and the future embraced at any given moment. Sheer duration of time cannot explain its movement, for there is no fixed amount of time that announces itself as the present. Just the contrary, that time passes means that measurement or observation is outside of time. If past and future cannot be figured in objective terms determined by duration, then they are more usefully taken as divergent dispositions, the past is lost and therefore melancholic, and the future has yet to take on any burden and is therefore joyful. Luhmann notes that the "present is to be experienced as melancholy joy, thus as a paradox" (42). The ambivalence in the present urges decision without resolution and leaves uncertainty in its wake. Yet the paradox in Luhmann is that risk is viewed as the "other side of the normal form" whose function is to "comprehend misfortune" (viii), whereas it would seem that he himself has established risk as the normal form for the passage of time.

Financialization, far from being the other side of the norm, establishes the routinization of risk. Risk becomes normative not so much because it rewards its adepts with success but more because the embrace of risk means one is embedded in the reality of the present. A risk taker is one who lives for the moment—the historical moment in which risk management ascends to the status of common sense. To be risk averse is to have one's life managed by others, to be subject to their miscalculations, and therefore to be unaccountable to oneself. Certainly the generalized suspicion toward expertise that runs through the financial self-help literature implies that it is immoral if not unethical for professionals to take money when they cannot do better than the market (meet the norm). The cautionary tales of the Motley Fool and the money drunk speak to the dangers of dependency even as they elevate particular forms of mutual interdependence. The Fool relies on risk-savvy individuals sharing information and constituting a common good for personal gain. The money drunk will shed debt dependency promoted by the credit industry by admitting that over which there is no control, the future. God is a one-figure investment club, a multiplicity in unity that encourages the constitution of a risk-managed self. For both the uninitiated and the addict, risk management is a daily practice of decision and affirmation, research and reflection. The faith that life can be known as the discrepancy from expected return renders risk routine.

Routinization of risk makes a particular historical and economic arrangement appear to be natural. This makes common sense out of what was hitherto nonsensical. Which matters appear dangerous and which should be ignored have been part of consensus arrangements in society, according to Mary Douglas and Aaron Wildavsky.[8] Mary Douglas has shown especially how natural dangers are related to moral defects. Where risk can be perceived, it is attributed as moral blame. The modern link to natural dangers shows up as technical and environmental risk. But now the morally polluted are those who won't take risks and are victims of lost opportunity with only themselves to blame. Douglas and Wildavsky are skeptical of the economists' claim to information processing as a seamless web in decision making. They note that most people are not good judges of probability and don't go out of their way to get information. They take up Herbert Simon's notion of "bounded rationality," which accepts limits to the amount of information that can be processed.[9] Financialization bounds rationality in a different direction. Surely, in an information-saturated world people cannot know everything. But still, decisions need to be authenticated when information is self-generated.

The point of Douglas and Wildavsky's work is to denaturalize risk by indicating how societies construct themselves through the means in which they select dangers. For example, those that articulate themselves through long-term goals will rely on the value of traditions to justify the imperative to stay the course despite immediate circumstances. This again places risk in a temporal formula. "The social past and social future are like a balance: if one is long, the other must be just as long; if the future is to be heavy, the past must be equally so. . . . The converse holds: a future that only has a short term is unmortgaged; its past has not been allowed to stake forward claims. Living in the present means inventing cutout mechanisms which prevent that future from being cluttered with a load of obligations" (87). So if financialization implies an extreme form of presentism, the sensibility of the 2001 tax cut so central to the early George W. Bush presidency is understandable more in terms of a truncated future discharged of obligation than merely a festival of greed. Or at least financialization would naturalize the present so that no future is imaginable and therefore no interest in it need be addressed through public policy.

Students of risk have been struck by the paradox that it flourishes amid affluence.[10] In silent conversation with those who have puzzled over stagnant satisfaction amid prosperity, the new climate of risk flourishes despite material improvements. As inequitable as the gains in wealth have been, so too, the distribution of risk has been uneven. The unevenness is captured by the term "at risk" which came into common parlance in the early 1980s to designate those who are objects of structural inequities. Instead of talking about economic exploitation, racial domination, or sexual oppression, the attribution of risk shifted the burdens of these exclusionary social effects to the groups themselves. Poverty and race could then become risk factors for failure. Demography and not social organization would serve to shape conditions of policy intervention and amelioration. Even though it was being popularized at the same time, the separation of financial risk from other risk types meant that failure to thrive could be a natural or cultural attribute but not a feature of the market as such. By describing negative outcomes of social life in terms of risk, unpredictabilities of the market like layoffs through downsizing could become integrated into the experience of the employed as an ongoing uncertainty that all would have to live with. The decline of welfare state perquisites, manifest in such mechanisms as time limits on welfare benefits, defines the postdeadline future as uncertain and deploys this uncertainty as an incentive to press people into the job market. Once there, they find that the same volatility applies. The shrinking of welfare rolls communicates to every citizen that there is "no free ride," meaning that all must take for themselves the responsibility for a safety net.

After enough years of public authorities' denials that they can take responsibility for the public good and security, people believe this to be the case and lose trust, not just in governmental but in institutional solutions (be they public or private) to social problems. Crime may be down, but insecurity is up. The self-help moves in welfare and finance are part of the same stratified risk climate advertised in the name of both government and corporate sponsor in which each is to find a personal management approach appropriate to her station.[11] While governments promoted privatization, both public and private sectors advanced the idea that no one can solve your problems but yourself. Experts continued to abound, but none could offer guarantees to future uncertainties. Integrating the future into the present could only leave room for more self-doubt, which in turn expanded the arena in which risk could serve as life's barometer. So long as risk was everywhere, failure could be imminent at any turn for any possible venture, whether it be health, education, employment, investment, or personal affection. No wonder it was hard to admit good times into the experiential vault. Pollsters would be as likely to record paranoia as pleasure.

In a world rendered into risk, self-knowledge, even of tangible improvements or movement toward goals, may not be sufficient to quell the anxieties of making uncertainty such intimate company with decision and evaluation. Deborah Lupton has surveyed meanings of risk and grasps well how its generalization presents a seemingly intractable problem that contrasts with the optimism of expanding certainty through more extensive knowledge:

> Compulsive self-monitoring is not consistent with uncertainty and ambivalence, for these allow no guidelines by which self-monitoring can take place. Indeed, "the very notion of 'risk' entails making calculable the incalculable or monitoring of contingency" (Lash 1993:6). People often feel, however, that knowledges about risk, including their own, are so precarious and contingent that they simply do not know what course of action to take. As a result, they may move between different risk positions at different times, sometimes attempting to control risk, at other times preferring a fatalistic approach that simply accepts the possibility of risk without attempting to avoid it.[12]

Though constant vigilance and doubt, will to control and fatalism, may not be logically consistent, their twinning produces the unreason of risk. Sartre understood that knowledge and nausea made inseparable bedfellows, but this insight seems to have slipped from the risk writer's cognition. Lupton acknowledges more than most of her colleagues that there are connotations of risk that are affirmative and designed to be embraced for self-betterment. For most, she observes, "risk is now a synonym for danger or hazard, and the early modern concept of a 'good risk' appears largely to have been removed from the vernacular, appearing only in the parlance of economic speculation" (148). Negatively, risk is marked on the body as deviant, abject, in a state of failure. The reversal relegates risk to the domain of pleasure, transgression, and transcendence. From sadomasochism to extreme sports, danger is turned into a valued means and ends. "The skilled performance of the dangerous activity" controls chaos and returns mental toughness (151). This is a pleasure that relies on its own modes of expertise and, in both instances, specialized sartorial accouterment. The embrace of risk becomes "part of the trajectory of self-actualization" (154). The journey may be carefully scripted beforehand and may require great preparation and skill acquisition that link the exceptional activity back to the reaffirmation of certain norms. No small surprise that wilderness experiences and other physical challenges can be incorporated into management training programs. The idea of taking a risk is a well-controlled catharsis. Here, risk is a substitute for the kinds of career mobility associated with lifelong commitment to a single firm's job ladder. Henceforth, advancement based on loyalty and performance will be replaced by "personal flexibility." The costs of these moves are borne by the individual, not by the company. "The notion is that once a person has reached a certain level in their career, they may need to take a risk—to move to another position, perhaps involving a cut in salary—in order to achieve long term goals" (156).

The ability to assume short-term loss for the promise of long-term gain is stock market rhetoric. Whereas one can divest from the stock market or move funds into other instruments, divestiture from the labor market is a more difficult trick. The analogy reinforces the credibility of both items in the comparison. But there is also a dis-analogy at work. The standard advice in investments is "Only front what you can afford to lose." But while a salary cut could be represented as money placed at risk, one cannot actually speculate with the forgone wages. Some might say that what is being gained is human capital, additional capacity to create value.[13] The sense in which this capacity acts as capital, however, is tenuous. The price of knowledge is set by the purchaser, and although knowledge can be expansive, for the individual who claims it nothing allows it to accumulate. Humans are to act as if they were capital by assuming the uncertainty of outcome without exercising control over the conditions of making wealth.

Perhaps the most affirmative associations of risk can be found in the arts, where novelty remains a fundamental evaluative criterion. In the arts, at least under the assumptions of Western modernism, departure from expected returns is the expectation. For an investor in the arts, there are no guarantees that esthetic risk will translate into financial gain, for departures from expectation still require institutional and critical recognition to signal success. For the artist as cultural figure, risk is part of creative being. Danger, uncertainty, volatility, marginality, extreme challenge, extraordinary skill—all these terms were applied approvingly to an artist's self-concept throughout the twentieth century. Artists are obliged to place themselves at risk, both of failure and of the unexpected, if a creative return is to be realized. Speaking of risk as a portrait of the artist is convenient in describing a personality type without predetermining the type or appearance of the artwork. This notion of individuality—a common personal disposition generating multiple formal outcomes—could be applied equally to the risk-taking artist or investor. Perhaps the most intriguing link between art and personal finance is the conjunctural one. During the past twenty-five years in which financial self-management has ascended, risk has become an esthetic value in a variety of artistic media. Just as risk got somatized for the neophyte Internet investor (can you sleep at night?), so too, the turn to the body that issued from 1970s feminist performance art and continues in contemporary dance foregrounds a figure of risk. For visual artists like Francis Bacon or Damien Hurst, the body is cut, eviscerated, or dissected. For Matthew Barney or Stellarc, it is the artist's own body that is rendered grotesque.

In either case the viewer is confronted by a body that is not unitary but, like a good portfolio, diversified. The interior of the body, like an obscure stock, can be undervalued and therefore relied upon for disproportionate exposure. One lineage of contemporary dance performance eschews the upright, centered, and gravity-defying techniques of ballet for weight-sharing partnerships among dancers. The technique, called contact improvisation, features rolling, lifting, and aerial transit from multiple bodily orientations. The improvisational approach leads to uncertain movement outcomes based upon often precarious interactions where dancers entrust their own body weight to another. As performances based in the traditions of contact improvisation developed increasing technical mastery, the ability and value multiplied for precarious and kinesthetically charged movement with the apparatus of an acrobat. This notion of risk joined the pleasure of the performer in executing a precarious move with the enjoyment of audiences watching bodies achieve unexpected configurations and capacities. Some choreographers, like Elizabeth Streb, have used acrobatic and gymnastic gear to intensify speed, lift, and intricacy of movement partnerships. There is danger in the physical risk of injury that dancers sustain, but agility serves as a prophylaxis. Whereas safe sex was to protect from death through some material separation of pleasure and danger, increased capacity for danger (by no means assuring avoidance of harm through injury) could be achieved through both technical and creative expansion.[14]

The pleasurable connotations of risk that govern art, sport, and leisure resonate with and may help to promote applications of risk where it was thought best avoided for the layperson. The spillover of risk from art to life was typically not proselytized by artists. Conversely, the generalization of the model of business risk to daily life has been a definite point of financializing acolytes. The confidence that business is the best model for all of human endeavor underwrites the neoliberal faith in privatization. In response to the proliferation of risk in the world in domains of economy, environment, and disease control have come proposals to transfer business "best practice" to all arenas.[15] If a best practice succeeds at accomplishing a particular task better than other approaches to the same problem, what happens when the specificity of the problem is removed? The ability to solve problems in a given context must be abstracted from the designation "best" so that the latter can travel to other domains. So it is the designation of best itself that resolves the problem of transferring an approach from one setting to another and begs the question of what made the practice so good in the first place. Like other managerialist calls for excellence, a best practice has "no content to call its own," but this property is precisely what allows the idea to travel so well and makes its applicability so difficult to refute.[16]

The claim to being contentless also abets the generalization of risk management to all domains of life. In one popularization of more technical approaches to decision based on costing out the effects of making one choice over another (decision trees), Dan Borge proclaims, "You are the risk manager of your own life and you must use your judgement in applying advice and information supplied by others."[17] A "personal balance sheet" derives well-being from the difference between assets and liabilities—these last two distinguished between financial, physical, intellectual, and emotional. An emotional asset would be free time or inner peace, while an emotional liability could be personal angst or spending time with unpleasant people. Intellectual and emotional currency may be most difficult to quantify, but utilitarian costs can still be applied. Accepting this risk calculus is paramount, not in order to make money at all costs, but "because rational human beings should care about *utility* not money in and of itself" (206). Risk management is presented as if it were the best approximation of human nature, not of corporate organization. "Corporate risk management techniques are practical but focus on the wrong objectives for a rational human being" (206).

But even for Borge, risk management has a clear provenance. To explain the concept, he has us in the shoes of a boss. "If you are not the chief executive officer (CEO) of a major corporation, imagine that you are" (10). After chapters "Grooming You to Be CEO," and offering "The View from the CEO's Chair," you're ready to leave the corporation you've headed "with a nice fat severance package" and "turn your attention to the most important risk management challenge of all—your life" (187). The ability to subordinate money to life presupposes having a lot of the former, just as the generalization of management comes from being first a manager. No wonder then that the account of risk management's proliferation focuses on where people are heading, not where they have (or haven't) come from. "The purpose of risk management is to *improve the future, not to explain the past*" (6). Without inequities of the past (or present), the future can be constructed as a shared domain, uncertain but not unimaginable, where action can increase the odds of good outcomes. The manager is not objective but interested; scientific methods and analysis are used to partisan ends; and judgment, feeling, and art are just as important to sound decision. Fact and logic are applied not to describe how the world is, but to determine what ought to be done to advance self-interest (9).

As an approach to life, risk is a hybrid of objectivity and subjectivity applied less to craft a future than to inhabit it with preferred outcomes. Improvement of the future offers a mode of conduct for the present that begs the question of what the future might be. A bit more insidiously, gazing toward the distant horizon allows the past to slip in as the actual determinant of fate. Forecasting, after all, is an extrapolation of data about what has already happened in order to project what things would be like if the world stayed the same. Anyone involved in the financial rather than existential side of risk management readily acknowledges these limitations to forecasting. The contentless risk is happy to move on from the numbers that begat it when counting on the future proves inconvenient.[18] Embracing the limits to science dovetails nicely with the suspicion toward experts that encourages the assimilation of their expertise. Risk necessitates a leap of faith into the present that the adoption of the experts' techniques but not their guarantees will pay off. But what exactly does this mean? Here the utilitarian narrative breaks off. Meaning is not its field.

Management of others does not assume that they are better off, only that results of efforts are knowable. Managed self-knowledge presupposes that the meaning of life is achievable through demonstrable goal attainment. The utilitarian worldview can be a terribly lonesome experience. In the rush to achieve personal attainments it is difficult to see that all are being reconciled to the same techniques for inhabiting the present. The rampant individualism of profit or maximization of ends disavows the very socialization upon which it depends. This was always the manager's secret, that others were to be relied upon to do the work. Now this secret is to be revealed to all the selves who risk planning the future.

Just as risk management underwent a populist migration from boardroom to living room, other models of selfhood have come tumbling out of financial markets. The shareholder and stakeholder are meant not only to infuse capitalism with its needed life blood, but to orient people as to how to live through the market. For example, Bruce Ackerman and Anne Alstott propose a "stakeholder society" in which each citizen is to be provided with venture capital of $80,000 to be used for any (useful) purpose. Like the risk manager, "they must take responsibility for their choices. Their triumphs and blunders are their own."[19] The stake is intended to ameliorate inequality of opportunity and curry capital into national investment in the "American ideal," to pursue happiness. Public guarantee of individual initiative will engender responsibility to the country, and citizens will be encouraged to return the capital upon their deaths. Stakeholding is meant as a "new master metaphor to displace the insurance analogy" (16) associated with the rapidly unraveling safety net of the discredited welfare state. In the language of risk management, insurance may protect against the prospect of future loss, but it denies the opportunity to use lost income (premiums) in the present for future gain.

Those who have capital can self-insure and take responsibility for their own risk. Ackerman and Alstott's tactical goal is economic citizenship through progressive taxation and guaranteed retirement income. Their strategic interest is to reinvigorate the belief in American national citizenship through government disbursement of risk. Without being granted a stake in the market, citizens will lose faith in the system. Economic citizenship is to be literalized as stock in America. Billing itself as liberal individualist, the stakeholder society claims that investment in self-interest, made possible through a national right, will generate a community ethos, "to repay their own debt by passing on their great heritage to the future" (44). It is not difficult to see how consistent this sense of time is with the financialized self.

For an investment to grow, the time medium must remain constant. A past (heritage) becomes future through the perpetual present of the individual. Whatever the political or practical obstacles to such proposals, what is most germane to financialization is the common belief that holding stock (here denominated in national currency and not any mix of corporations) is socially binding. Individualism is the manifest form of this sociality. The belief is that the self expands when the stock accrues value. Personal choice is credited with the expansion. In practice, stock ownership is a decision over the disposition of wealth that is yielded to others. The individual account is credited with the gains made by the corporation. Pooled wealth and common ownership makes this possible, but the social basis of individual success is disavowed as a condition of individual identity formation.

What are the kinds of sociality that stockholding engenders? Rather than arguing that individualism constitutes a kind of false consciousness for the investment driven, it is more intriguing to trace the kinds of social integuments that make this particular kind of selfhood possible. A look at the financial self makes individualism difficult to sustain as a process when the making of each decision is done through others. Perhaps this is the meaning of the future emphasis: the difference from the present stands for a connection with others. The future cannot be predicted, but the orientation toward it, expressed as risk, is what gives intent to otherwise random outcomes. The notion that the market cannot be predicted, only played, is tied to Bernard Malkiel's popular account of the "random walk down Wall Street," first issued in 1973. That the future has an indeterminate or random relation to prior occurrences is explained by the "efficient market theory." "It holds that the stock market is so good at adjusting to new information that no one can predict its future course in a superior manner. Because of the actions of the pros, the prices of individual stocks quickly reflect all the news that is available. Thus, the odds of selecting superior stocks or anticipating the general direction of the market are even. Your guess is as good as that of the ape, your stockbroker, or even mine."[20]

Though the market is often anthropomorphized as an individual creature that heats or cools, a bull or a bear, the lone figure stands in for the actual community of decision whose collective intelligence outweighs any single person's capacity. When the stock market is the province of professionals, typical decisions incorporate the highest levels of expertise. In that sense, no one can be smarter than all the smart people put together. Yet the result of this well-gathered expertise is to render it moot, so that anyone picking a stock—you, me, and ape—despite one's individual relation to that collected intelligence, joins in its effects and opportunities. Needless to say, this treatment, like the others on stock picking, begs the question of whether having capital in the first place bears upon access to the means of participation. Like the lottery, it's a dollar and a dream. The claim may ring hollow as a democratic promise, but describes better the means through which the market socializes participation, by making its particular effects of gain or loss only available through a communal effort.

The idea of randomness suggests that rather than celebrating individual choice, the efficient market is indifferent to sheer acts of will to reward its kindnesses. Of course, were this the whole story, none of the books discussed here would have been written. By definition, if a series of outcomes are random, a certain number of results will significantly depart from the norm. But in the hands of the efficient market, what slips outside the norm is due, not to chance, but to risk. Malkiel again: "Common sense attests that some people can and do beat the market. It's not all chance. Many academics agree; but the method of beating the market, they say, is not to exercise superior clairvoyance but rather to assume greater risk. Risk, and risk alone, determines the degree to which returns will be above or below average, and thus decides the valuation of any stock relative to the market" (200). This is both a hypothesis supported by some

evidence and a self-justification that those with more to
venture have more to gain.[21]

For the purposes of this discussion, the question is not
whether such claims are tautological (market beaters beat
the market), but the relation between self and other presupposed by this adoption of risk. While the willingness to
accept risk is seen as purely subjective ("can you sleep at
night?), the consequence of risk acceptance is that the actions of others take hold of your fate. To be undisturbed by
risk is to accept this sociality to a greater degree. This tremu-
lous breach between inner and outer worlds is certainly not
part of the identification of the risk-taking investor. The dis-
avowal of the very sociality needed to abide the world of exchange is helped along by the antigovernment stance that
the risk tolerant are invited to assume. Malkiel too has his
"fitness manual for random walkers," designed to promote
restful nights through exercises that can serve as a "strategy
to foil the tax collector" (294). To exercise financial self-
management is to see one's own gains as emerging against
those bodies that represent the kind of social interdependence that made profit taking possible in the first place. Like
risk itself, the demands of others represented by the tax collector are not to be avoided, but successfully managed.

Socializing Finance

People are socialized into the world of finance both by participation in investment activity and by exposure to popular media saturated with news, images, and the attractions
of money management. While the long stock market run
was the harbinger of financialization, the discipline and desire evoked by the appeal to self-management have outlived
the recent market downturn. Because the personal com-

puter is so intricately bound with financialization as a medium of participation and the most sturdy reference to what the supposed new economy is all about, the fluorescence of online investing seems as tangible a measure as any of the larger phenomenon's reach into daily life. That so many people lost so much money has had an impact on the volume of trading on-line, the volume of assets, and the share of total trading engaged in. Yet despite a decline in all these areas that corresponded to the spring 2000 implosion of Internet stocks, the actual number of on-line brokerage accounts continued to rise in the year after the bubble burst, topping 20 million by early 2001. This is nearly three times the number of accounts only three years earlier. This growth in participation is not confined to the elderly or the affluent. More than a third of those trading are under 34, and roughly an equal proportion have annual incomes under $50,000.[22]

These figures all refer to accounts and not persons, and even if they did count persons, more than half of those who own stocks would not be trading on-line. But adopting the assumptions of risk tolerance cannot be reduced to whether or not people click buy or sell on their computers. The lessons of finance are learned through risk exposure, which can orient belief through any number of means. Hence, one may have to be in the market in order to win, but one need not be an investor, on-line or otherwise, to be subject to or called upon to take up finance's way of life. While the surfeit of dot.com ads do mean to increase stock valuation by getting people to visit a "cool site" (at least it seems so on TV), the media exposure to the world of finance is far more diffuse, extending from ads for financial services or new media, to increasingly prominent place given to financial news in conventional media, to those channels dedicated to the financial world. It is growth of this last arena for living with finance on a daily basis that references the kind of mediated participation discussed here.

The most successful of the dedicated finance news broadcasts is CNBC, founded in 1989. By 1992 it still had only 50,000 viewers. Eight years later it was seen in 150 million households in seventy countries.[23] The ideal viewer for CNBC would seem to be the hyperactive day trader, willing to move on every slip of an indicator or innocuous rumor. When decomposed into its constituent elements, the stock market is only volatility, an endless stream of numbers moving up or down. This stream of individual stock prices is what frames the CNBC screen and acts as its metronome, while talking heads behind computer screens try to give account to the endless movement and to lean toward what may come. Keeping in mind that only a minority of individual investors trade more than twice a month, the bulk of those millions of households are not acting on information broadcast to them, but taking the electronic ticker tape as a drone to life. It is in this area that the seepage may be far more significant into what counts as participation. News broadcasts are not simply a corporate assessment of what it is worth knowing; they are also the medium through which people imagine that they are living in the same world.

In June 2001, when the Federal Reserve cut interest rates for the sixth time in so many months, it was front-page news, and was also featured on the personal finance links of major web servers like Netscape Navigator. A byline posted by CBS's on-line financial news, MarketWatch.com, in the "Getting Personal" column read, "A Mood Elevator: Fed cuts marginally lower loan rates but boost spirits. The Fed's rate cuts this year have provided a stimulant for consumer spending, but it's been more of a psychological boost than a monetary one, experts say."[24] What the article does not explain is how adjustments to monetary policy that have little direct financial impact on consumer debt become enhancements to the national psyche. The claim is that the Fed acts not for other banks but directly for the people. At this point, the news is not simply covering the action of a government agency but transmitting the intended policy effect. If the Fed is now placed to feel the people's pain and offer palliative cocktails, then clearly monetary policy is being asked to do what the safety net of the welfare state was once meant to do, namely, allow every citizen to be assured that people are being looked after, included, and cared for should the violence of the market get them down. Not only does government seek to assure ground for participation in a democracy where finance rules by means of adjustments to finance, but the terms of critique that exemplify public discussion are expressed financially as well.

The combination of greater public participation in finance and its concomitantly larger presence as policy signals what Daniel Gross calls the democratization of money, which he takes to be what makes the 1990s different from the decade before:

> The age of the Masters of the Universe has given way to an
> era in which the masters—the CEOs—are increasingly being
> forced to answer the servants, and in which the fiercest critics
> of capitalism clip bond coupons and collect dividends. The
> place of money and stockholding in politics has undergone a
> similar shift in the 1990s: The precinct of money, traditionally
> rock-ribbed Republican, has become one in which Democrats
> are more comfortable. In many ways, the democratization of
> money has led to the Democratization of money. As the 1990s
> wore on, Democrats, and, in particular, the Clinton adminis-
> tration, grew not only to tolerate and appreciate the markets
> but even to love and embrace them. (80)

For Gross, the dimensions of this criticism are certainly not fierce enough to call capitalism itself into question, but relate to the kind of shareholder politics discussed earlier in this chapter. Gross offers "humble capitalism" as the thing that can save us from an "arrogant capitalism" which, he is concerned, could end the game altogether. The notion of arrogant capital comes from a book of that name published in 1994 by Kevin Phillips. Phillips lays responsibility for such arrogance on the "financialization of America." For Phillips, a one-time conservative who became an ardent chronicler of inequality, finance has gone awry and turned its back on America. "Finance has not simply been spreading into every nook and cranny of economic life; a sizable portion of the financial sector, electronically liberated from past constraints, has put aside old concerns with funding the nation's long-range industrial future, has divorced itself from the precarious prospects of Americans who toil in the factories, fields, or even suburban shopping malls and is simply feeding wherever it can."[25] Capital is not intrinsically arrogant, but it becomes so when it loses its productive vocation. In this reckoning, financialization is concentration of wealth without any accompanying socialization.

Gross, writing with a similar sensibility but a few years later when finance was more thoroughly woven into popular culture, instead wants to rescue finance from its own evils. He explains that the humblers want to cap executive pay through stockholder's proxy, in an intimation that socialized ownership has made large corporations susceptible to democratic kinds of public rebuke. As examples he cites the Boston-based group of monied stockholders who have an older sensibility called Responsible Wealth, as well as a proxy battle undertaken by the Louisiana Teachers Retire-

ment System against the compensation package of Occi-
dental Petroleum CEO Ray Irani, whose pay swelled to $100
million while his company underperformed the market average (198). By this reckoning, the managers of public funds
speak the vox populi by defining maldistributed compensation as a matter of the public interest. Leave it to the good
capitalists to police and exorcize those whose hands dipped
too deeply into the well. Jesse Jackson imagined that his
Wall Street Project, founded in 1997, could be a purveyor of
racial justice, by sharing the bully pulpit with President
Clinton to "instruct the financial services industry on the
glories of diversity" (82).

Gross assures us that there is nothing radical in humility:
"It's not envious or socialistic to insist that millionaires and
billionaires earn their paychecks, just as is required of welfare mothers and minimum wage workers. In this investor
nation, when seemingly everybody tracks the performance
of stocks, there's nothing wrong with making public examples of avaricious CEOs who break faith with the public by
taking compensation they don't deserve. It's a matter of *responsibility* and *accountability*—words that resonate with com-
passionate conservatives as much as they do with New Democrats" (198). So the democratization of money has more to
do with the collapse of difference between the parties than
with the Democrats' triumph, an observation that turned
out to have its own prescience. In the investor nation it's
"from each according to one's ability, to each according to
one's just desserts." This is indeed not socialism, but a new
justification for inequality, on the basis of its own accountability. Presumably all can enter the fray of stockholding politics, and Gross cites the case of striking steelworkers who
finally prevailed on Wheeling-Pittsburgh Steel Corporation
by taking their case to stockholders and getting asset man-

agers to pressure the company (64). The same logic applied within the Clinton White House, where former Wall Street investment banker and then Treasury Secretary Robert Rubin provided the president with daily briefings on the disposition of the bond market (92). Financial and political decisions were to dance to the same tune on the same stage.

Participation of this sort does not happen of its own accord. The participants must share certain norms and techniques that allow them to engage in common activity that is mutually understandable and consequential. For anyone who has taken a look at a stock proxy statement that comes in the mail, it can sure seem that the arcane prevails. The divide between expert and lay opinion is sustained linguistically. If responsibility and accountability were to reign over the investment roost, the language of account could not reside in a tower of Babel; it would itself have to be democratized. Financial literacy would have to cut both ways: common people would need to speak fondly of money, and money talk would have to stop speaking in tongues. Such a literacy campaign was orchestrated not by the Education Department (although it took part), but by the principal regulator of the financial markets, the Securities and Exchange Commission. Its humble hero, the morally vituperative Arthur Levitt who valiantly took on fourteen-year-old Jonathan Lebed, would become headmaster in a mission of national pedagogy. Said he, "I want to encourage people who have a very small stake in our economy to learn more about investments" (130).

To achieve this goal, Levitt made publicly accessible the government-mandated documents that corporations are required to file on their activities. Because companies were required to file electronically, the data were accessible but, until the early 1990s, sold to a private firm that in turn sold the data to information retailers with Wall Street clientele. In 1994 a web site was created to make the service, the Electronic Data Gathering, Analysis, and Retrieval system (EDGAR), freely available. Soon the site was being accessed by 50,000 people a day, and by 2000, one million documents were being downloaded daily from EDGAR. Companies must report gains and losses, general business strategies, and earnings projections based on risk. For example, in its 2000 filing, Microsoft reported, in the midst of the antitrust suit filed against it, "There are government regulation and investigation risks along with other general corporate legal risks."[26]

Once again, this quotation suggests that the very presence of the state can yield negative outcomes which, for Microsoft and others, are quantified in earnings estimates. Gross argues that, when EDGAR became a public service, "the mechanics of disclosure had been democratized. But Levitt also believed it was crucial that the *content* of disclosure change, because the documents, laden with boilerplate legalisms and often intentionally obfuscatory prose, were frequently unintelligible to the millions of new investors flooding into the markets. 'I was convinced that few people read prospectuses or annual reports, and wanted to do something about it, so I had to start with language. . . . It's my hope to have prospectuses begin to speak a new language— the English language'" (130–31).

The SEC issued its own style manual for prospectuses, *The Plain English Handbook: How to Create Clear SEC Disclosure Documents,* and in 1997 codified linguistic regulations for corporate documents submitted to the SEC. The *Handbook* has a preface by Warren Buffett, who swears that the absence of legalese will "make my life easier" (who knew it was so hard?). Plain speech attacks the rhetoric of finance and law while privileging the positions of experts, for they remain the authors whom others must read. The meaning of the new language is happily defined. "Plain English means analyzing and deciding what information investors need to make informed decisions before words, sentences or paragraphs are considered. A plain English document uses words economically and at a level the audience can understand."[27]

Perhaps it is no surprise that when words are used "economically" the result is transparency. Information, here, is prior to language and still requires expert selection and translation. Transparency, it turns out, is not necessarily intrinsically friendly to clarity. As one recent report put it, where transparency is concerned, "the mantra is 'more is better.' More data, more reports and more proof. . . ."[28] Profusion is information's natural state, and the experts must reengineer themselves if they want to hold on to their expertise. The surfeit of numbers would abide an opposite economy from the parsimony of words.

Such state directives on the proper use of language might have given another inflection to the term "politically correct," but it was never applied. Financial transparency would have its correlate in linguistic clarity, although both could readily degenerate into confusion. Whether or not serif typefaces, use of boldface type rather than all caps, and "growth" instead of "capital appreciation" would actually give the undercapitalized command of the market could remain an object of speculation. Accessible words and fonts could pass for understanding, just as access to information was the best proxy for fully vested powers of decision making and participation. To the extent, however, that government regulation now meant teaching people how to speak plainly, the meaning of state intervention would achieve a reach unimaginable under the loathed sign of big government. Levitt was suggesting that the function of the state was to teach power how to talk to the people such that they too would believe they were invested.

Such newly proclaimed powers of state and capital did not come without their own complications. The shareholder/stakeholder model of the "investor nation" renders the corporation the ideal citizen held to the highest standards of being an ethical subject. Whatever the success or limitations of individual stock proxy efforts to redistribute wealth or achieve racial justice, it may be more useful to understand the context in which they come about than to have confidence in their generalizability. At least one contradictory consequence of this newly defined corporate ethos is that corporations may now need to be answerable to political demands that the good old welfare state was supposed to shoulder for them. Much has been said about the depletion of governmental mandates to attend to the common good that issue from neoliberal pleas for privatization.

Private firms gain from government actions that were once seen to be morally corrupting. The other side of privatization, beyond the publicly assisted extension of profitable activities, is that corporations now must shoulder some of the ethical and political burden associated with being models for a newly unified public and private life. If the state had once drawn the heat for the disappointments of the system or the injustices of the market, under the new transparency the company would be asked to stand naked for all the world to see. Granted, in proxy battles only shareholders are entitled to become stakeholders and therefore actually participate in decision making. At minimum, there is some dissonance between actual entitlements to participation based on ownership and symbolic claims based on metaphorical notions of citizenship. Companies, unlike gov-

ernments, only need to listen to their owners, but ownership is becoming increasingly interlocking. If it is good business to be clear, as the *Handbook* suggests, and if clarity engenders participation, how is capital to limit the demands
placed upon it?

Peter Drucker, ever prescient in looking out for the shoals
into which management might run, saw this one coming in
the mid-1970s as pensions were being reconfigured. Drucker's *The Unseen Revolution* proclaimed the United States "the
first truly 'Socialist' country," because workers, through their
pension funds, "own at least 25% of its equity capital, which
is more than enough for control."[29] In Drucker's reckoning,
socialism was introduced by then head of General Motors
Charles Wilson in 1950 to "blunt union militancy by making visible the workers' stake in company profits and company success" (6) and to pit younger members in the bar-
gaining unit concerned with wages against senior members
with an interest in maximizing pensions. Wilson thought
that simply distributing GM stock to workers would be financially unsound and dishonest, as workers should not be de-
ferring wages to the company they worked for and needed
to have their futures protected from the fate of a single enterprise. Pensions should be tied to expanding productive
capacity broadly distributed, and not to a specific debt claim
to future income. This was, of course, before single firms
like Enron would claim this kind of diversification associated with the market as a whole for themselves, and invite
their workers to contribute to their future tragedy.

More than two decades later, Wilson's appreciation for
how to undercut labor militancy and free his own firm from
demands for local control was enshrined in the 1974 Employees Retirement Security Act (ERISA). ERISA provided
the groundwork for the shift to defined-contribution over

defined-benefit pension plans that Drucker accurately predicted in different terms. Support for the economic needs of
a gerontocracy had to avoid undermining the political interests of all others. Consequently, policy objectives focused
on maximizing the increase of capital formation to pay for
the ever-expanding numbers of future retirees, together with
protecting their future income against erosion caused by inflation. With ownership interests oriented toward pension
accounts, Drucker argues, "as the pension trust becomes the
means to organize economic performance for social needs,
inflation can no longer even be defended economically"
(196–97). Because unemployment does not compromise the
pension funds themselves, Drucker proclaims it no longer a
threat to the principal interest of society (197).

The passage from Keynesian to monetarist social policy
is here framed as a kind of socialism. Drucker's equation of
ownership with control was certainly not borne out by corporate raiders who dismantled companies for immediate
gains and CEOs who gorged themselves on the stocks of the
companies they headed. As pension funds grew, greater decision-making authority over the nation's wealth was concentrated among captains of commerce, not the lieutenants
of labor. But Drucker did understand clearly that pension
politics were meant to counter the organizational powers of
labor, and in that respect, at least until recently, they proved
enormously effective. The relationship between ownership
and control is nowhere as direct as Drucker implies. The fact
of workers being the source of productive wealth does not
by itself make them wealthy, nor do their contributions to
the funds of investable capital convert them into capitalists.
In both cases, the appropriation of wealth amassed through
the contributions of so many require active political re-
direction.

The socialization of ownership like that of labor does not guarantee any given political expression, but it does make a range of issues hitherto reserved for high finance available for popularization. This is the other political implication of financialization. Labor's struggle for a living wage has been insightfully linked by Lawrence B. Glickman to the creation of consumer society. He suggests that workers redefined wages from a form of slavery in their nineteenth-century conception to becoming the means through which the market might be reshaped to meet their needs such that consumption could become a domain of emancipation.[30] Consumerism was not simply a co-optation of labor but an elaboration of workerist politics. Similar arguments are now being adduced for pension politics.

It is precisely the link between wages and pensions that labor unions negotiate or strike over, but that also privileges unions organizationally as addressing the socialization of finance and labor in concert. Unions have taken on the shareholder/stakeholder frameworks to influence both private investment orientations and public policy. The AFL-CIO has instituted the Center for Working Capital to coordinate these efforts. The center conducts research and educational seminars on investment activism, and brings together labor-oriented consultants and fund managers. In an effort to draw together some of the threads of Drucker's unseen socialism, these unionists are crafting organization and strategy that would shift nominal ownership of the $7 trillion in pension funds to certain forms of control over capital:

> At the end of the day, worker capital can organize itself, the regulatory environment can improve, and our efforts can become more focused on forwarding our view of value. Yet worker-owners will not be effective agents of change, until the worker-owner view of value drives the allocation of capital

through markets or firm decisions. That is the final and most difficult challenge facing worker capital today. One of the distinctive characteristics of worker capital's agenda is the wide range of responses to managerial and market behavior, including investment screening, informal dialogue, shareholder proposals, and independent-director candidacies. Yet worker capital will be a consequential market force only to the extent that it can decisively influence both large and small transactions.[31]

The initial gains of these efforts have been assessed as largely "political rather than economic," insofar as they have influenced the thinking of institutional fund managers and projected labor symbolically as contesting boardroom decisions about how capital circulates.[32] Seven trillion dollars is without question a huge sum, but it is sobering to think that this was also the amount of money lost as a result of the burst Internet bubble. If stock market volatility is considered to have more decisive economic impact than any particular approach to investment could, then perhaps the emphasis should properly be a political one. When value itself is reconsidered as something that issues from labor, then something more fundamental is being proposed than a product that takes into account the needs of its consumers, which is the conventional trajectory of the shareholder perspective.

Typically, executive compensation would be considered excessive when it compromised dividend payments or the values of shares. When the view of value is oriented not by maximizing share price, but by a labor-promoting "allocation of capital," the stakes for holding stock are considerably raised. The principle of private ownership of economic capacity separates the stakes of labor that makes the stuff we live on, from the modulations of price of those products attributed to the market. In conventional labor-organizing terms, this meant that labor could seek a greater slice, through pay raises, of the value of what it had produced. The questions of what got produced, who it was made for, what importance there would be to invest in making one thing or another, all those considerations were outside of labor's purview.

Working capital may begin with selection of companies that tolerate unions, keep shops open, don't lay off workers, pay living wages, don't discriminate, or even temper their environmental impact. After a slow start in the early 1980s, socially screened mutual funds like Domini Social Equity Fund, Citizens Trust, Trillium Asset Management, and the Calvert Group were generating returns that compared favorably to conventional funds, and by 1998 they held $2.2 trillion in assets.[33] Such funds typically screen out or exclude corporations involved in tobacco, gambling, or nuclear power. This policy is consistent with the negative choice usually meant by market freedom. The more provocative question would be, "When would considerations of value from labor's viewpoint actually bear on the design of the whole social landscape, shifting from questions of what gets produced to considerations of what production is for?" The presence of labor's view of value in the midst of capital's hitherto jealously guarded prerogative makes such considerations possible within the seemingly innocent guise of shareholder value.

That capital has become so thoroughly speculative has meant that it has come to rely for its wealth not only on taking labor from workers, but also on returning for a second helping. The growth of consumer credit, defined-contribution pensions, and other securities speaks to capital's unspoken dependence on labor's ability to make capital available for investment. The difference is that, while wages may be set socially, they are disbursed individually. As working capital, labor's deferred wages, pensions, and other investments are pooled, and they continue to exist in that social form even as individuals draw from their accounts. The rubric of consumer choice emerged to channel workers' use of their wages into productive ends. Now, that logic is being extended to the allocations of capital, which must remain social decisions. Insofar as those decisions become politicized in any direction, it may be difficult to govern the future directions that they could entertain. Screening out bad companies or selecting out bad commodities does individualize social decisions at the same time that it poses their very sociality. When capital itself must be marketed as a consumer good, it puts its privacy at risk.

Not all capital is tied up in the stock market. Diversification is standard advice for any investor's portfolio. Other forms of property once thought sacredly private are becoming socialized in the manner of stocks. The observation that common ownership of stock compromised some of the perquisites of the entrepreneur was made long before Drucker noted the socialist creep in pensions. At the dawn of the modern joint-stock corporation, Karl Marx, writing in the third volume of *Capital,* spoke of the "abolition of capital as private property within the framework of capitalist production itself."[34] In this process the advent of stockholding moves "toward the conversion of all functions in the reproduction process which still remain linked with capitalist property, into mere functions of associated producers, into social functions" (437).

By "reproduction process" Marx means both keeping conditions for making money going, keeping wealth on the move so that there can be more of it—the profit imperative—and maintaining a basis for people to live so that the work required to create wealth can get done. For Marx, capital's big dilemma is that it depends on labor to generate value but then finds that very dependence an obstacle to its further expansion. If workers need places to live, ways of getting to work, ways of taking care of children while they're at work, and the like, these needs will have to be paid for with individual and social wages (through taxes) that reduce potential profits. From the perspective of the stock market, capital moves in and out of individual companies fleeing loss in pursuit of gain. For labor, this disinvestment is from labor itself and from the costs of reproducing it, whether directly as compensation or indirectly as taxation.

Labor has always been on the move but has never enjoyed capital's mobility. As capital spreads, so does its dependence on labor, and so does any individual become tied in to the labor of others. The prosaic examples are the number of hands that may have touched a person's breakfast before it came to the table or handled the garments that drape our skin. In these examples, what is personal involves more and more people spread farther and farther apart. The same might be said for the Internet itself. It is not simply that a click connects those who are otherwise separated, but that using a computer assumes the involvement of so many who built it, maintain its networks, and sustain the environments in which it is housed. This socialization of labor means that the greater the experience of personal choice, the more the interdependence on unknown others. The same is the case for the socialization of capital. But now capital has nowhere to go but back into the hands of the very social functions it had tried to be free from in order expand wealth. The speculative turn would seem to be one outcome of this newly imposed claustrophobia. Capital's expansion abets not only itself, but also the interconnections of ownership. As more and more forms of property become socialized, however, ownership will be spread everywhere by means of common shares that associate people who can make a claim on capital.

The significant development to replace individual with social ownership of more and more kinds of property falls to securitization. Stocks are one form of security, but in the past two decades more and more kinds of debt are being bundled together and sold as securities. Securitization links all manner of property and receivables together under the same umbrella. Consider the following list offered in *A Primer on Securitization:* "Most new home mortgages and growing numbers of multifamily and commercial property mortgages are being funded by conversion into securities. Car loans and leases, credit card receivables, boat loans, mobile home loans, home equity loans, small business loans, student loans, problem loans, Third World debt, and even delinquent municipal tax liens also have been securitized by originators and Wall Street."[35] Notice that the list is as happy to subsume the personal as the political, the local as the foreign, the public as the private. All are to receive equal treatment in the conversion "from illiquid individual loans or debt instruments which cannot be sold readily to third-party investors into liquid, marketable securities."[36] Liquidity means denying property its attachments to individual person or particular place.

Not only will assets be free to move, but they can also achieve unfettered amalgamation whose only demarcation is price. Further, the link between business as a capacity for ownership and their particular lines of business is to be broken, so that firms of all sorts can become securities houses for myriad forms of debt. This socialization of ownership is called disintermediation because it replaces one set of intermediaries, banks, with others. For those others, the gains are nothing short of revolutionary:

> A revolution has occurred in the way the borrowing needs of consumers and businesses are met. The historic use of financial

intermediaries to gather deposits and lend them to those seeking funds is being supplemented and even replaced by securitization processes that bypass traditional intermediaries and link borrowers directly to money and capital markets. A complex array of loan originators, funders, securities conduits, credit enhancers, investment bankers, and domestic and global investors are displacing traditional portfolio lenders, local thrifts, and banks. Deregulation and the competition it fosters has atomized rather than concentrated finance in America. (1)

A curious form of atomization this, when half of the home loans, a fifth of the car loans, and a quarter of the credit card debt has been securitized, according to this author, Leon T. Kendall. Interestingly, his comments came in 1996 on the cusp of a wave of mergers and acquisitions in the financial services industry that have come because of the very displacement of traditional banking services he described. Straddling the 1999 Gramm-Leach-Bliley Act that deregulated financial services, between 1997 and 2000 there were more than 400 securities-firm combinations totaling $300 billion. The average deal size increased from $100 million in 1995 to $2.4 billion in 2000.[37] It would seem that the concentration of ownership that deregulation and competition allow has fostered atomization of possession while more and more are brought into the race. That the investors in these securities come from around the globe is particularly significant for those patterns of intermediation that appear to root ownership in neighborhoods or community—namely, savings banks and thrifts. Lost, however, through such disintermediation was the claim that people could invest not only in their own home, but also in a belief in capital's fidelity.

Jurisdictional and juridical differences limit the creation of cross-national real estate securities that would be wholly indifferent to place, but there are no constraints to who may invest in these securities. There is no reason to wax nostalgic for local masters, but this story of emancipation is hardly free from self-interest. To take one example, global banker John Reed, head of the premerged Citibank, proclaimed securitization "the substitution of more efficient public capital markets for less efficient, higher cost, financial intermediaries" (2). Another example: Real Estate Investment Trusts (REITs), were created by an act of Congress in 1960 to allow small investors into real estate speculation. REITs carried no minimum investment and had to return at least 90 percent of their income as dividends. For thirty years they were used largely as tax shelters and could not operate the properties whose titles they held. The 1986 Tax Reform Act eliminated those restrictions, and the building glut and savings and loan debacle of the 1980s dried up existing funds for new investment. REITs were reinvented in the 1990s as publicly traded companies. In a decade, volume quadrupled to $300 billion, and REITs became a standard component of diversified portfolios.[38]

Securitization, in general, claims to democratize access to investments that may once have required high minimums or limited partnerships. It also promises to increase returns over independent ownership (REITs averaged double what the appreciation for a single family home was) and to reduce capital costs through competition over interest rates. Securitization is meant to control risk by spreading it around and, like all market transactions, to increase efficiency. Increased efficiency is said to derive from greater volume and lower costs per unit. At the same time, many more nibble at the trough—among them, loan originators, rating agencies that evaluate risk, credit enhancers that insure against default, the tax-exempt trust that purchases the loans, and the underwriter or investment bank that prices and markets the securities. Prices can now fluctuate daily on the basis of trades, and the securities can be offered through a variety of terms and rates. Efficiency also comes from deregulation, which in this case meant Bank of America and other Wall Street investment houses lobbying successfully to get taxes removed from their transactions.

Risk abatement seeks safety in numbers. A decline in housing prices in one place can be compensated for elsewhere. Pooling large numbers of properties allows for the kinds of averaging on which the risk assessments are based. Individual fate is exchanged for a perspective on the whole. Also traded off is the relation between possession and self-mastery. While the sale of personal financial information has raised all manner of hackles over what constitutes privacy, ownership of that bastion of inner peace, the home, would seem a more decisive blow to the relation between one's personal living space and the entitlements of ownership. Now that ownership is so thoroughly spread around, far more can partake of the entitlements of others. When one holds a security, the title is to no single thing, but to an aggregate of ownership designed to eliminate the differences that particular conditions of possession can make (whether flood or default). Property becomes a general or abstract category when the distinction between the personal and commercial is blurred. Household consumption was the means through which social labor was translated into individual experience through possession of what one could call one's own.

Securitization is the new millennium's version of eighteenth-century Enclosure Acts. Whereas peasants had to be physically removed from common lands to dispossess them of property, now dispossession breeds commons without anyone needing to be moved anywhere. Possession has been rendered liquid so that it can be revalued daily. The active pulse of money in motion is the medium through which occasions arise to move physically from place to place as a job or home can no longer bear the demand for increased value placed upon it. Expanded capacity for risk tolerance is crucial to the liquidity of the personal, the willingness to dispossess oneself in order to recombine with opportunities for greater return elsewhere. Individual gain comes not only with a price, but with an expanded association, a rebundling, a willingness to live opportunity through those unbeknownst to oneself.

Socialization of risk through securitization of property not only ties people together, but makes life more volatile as well. Not only is property bundled together to control its fate, but it is also parcelized and decomposed to isolate its constituent uncertainties. Derivatives are the financial product line meant to hedge against unwanted outcomes by separating out components of a good or service that would be subject to variable outcomes. An example would be to fix the price of oak needed to fill an order of tables, or to set an exchange rate when the finished product might be shipped overseas. Such hedges against unwanted fluctuations in price tied to or derived from another item, derivatives, have been used for centuries as kinds of insurance. In their current incarnation, they have notoriously been used for high-stakes speculation.

Unlike the humble REITs, hedge funds often require million-dollar minimums and can fail spectacularly, as with Long Term Capital Management, the hedge fund mentioned in Chapter 1 that went into receivership in 1998 through the complex mathematics of Nobel Prize–winning economists. With $4.8 billion in capital, the firm put down payments on contracts that leveraged $120 billion to its balance sheet that was in turn connected to $1.3 trillion worth of assets through derivatives. Massive currency fluctuation in Russia and Asia due to sudden capital flight in the summer of 1998 forced the firm to pay out half its funds, in turn instantly doubling the ratio between its actual capital and its obligations ($2.3 billion to cover the $120 billion).[39] By flinging ownership far and wide, strangers come to control each other's fate, and the immediate conditions for responding to risk vary greatly. That the investment instrument provides no resistance to liquidation means that suddenly what was meant to spread risk around can extravagantly concentrate it.

Taking a long view on the advent of risk culture internationally, Richard Minns observes that the highly touted capital markets reflect an "innate confusion," namely, "They are supposed to *reduce* risk, not increase it." He goes on: "The idea of a new 'risk culture' is, in practice, similar to the concept of flight capital discussed earlier—it is an analogous reaction to the problems of bank capital and lending, or of committing capital to specific long-term liabilities. The increase in liquidity—the ability to sell or exit—acts against the interests of long-term investment because it leads to attempts to out-guess the market rather than understanding the long-term productive capacity of companies or countries."[40]

The confusion between reducing and increasing risk may turn out to be endemic to risk culture. Certainly, the attention to proving the safety of speculative activity has been a feature of legitimating financial markets for popular participation since the Great Depression. Participation in those markets has both a narrowly ideological aspect (getting people to believe that capitalism will deliver their future) and a narrowly economic one (creating capital out of labor a second time around through use of worker's savings). But a risk culture is not simply a means of tricking people into thinking they are safer or better off when their lives are hedged while in practice they are at risk. When risk is culture, life is lived to control outcomes and embrace uncertainty. Gains may or may not be realized, but appreciation is far more difficult to attain. If the confusion is not simply financial hucksterism passing as advice or information flows overloading the circuits of transparency, what accounts for the dizziness that accompanies personal risk management?

In this chapter, two processes have been discussed through which risk becomes the world. To be more precise, there are two senses in which socialization has been understood. The first is the common sociological meaning whereby people are brought into conformity with the assumptions of a given society. Although no grammar book for social codes is handed out at birth, the rules of the game are to be learned by playing. Since no bells go off when socialization of this sort is achieved, lessons are usually made out of failures to fit with unstated expectations. Just as grammar is noticed when mistakes are made, rules and norms are affirmed through their myriad deviations. Hence in the sociologies of risk we learn of danger and uncertainty, moral pollution and threat. Facing these risks, wrestling them to the ground, we are united (or divided as the case may be). This description makes for a nice fable of how society works by rule of law. With respect to finance, such fables are powerful indeed, whether they be of the natural sort (numeracy), of a more social Darwinian sort (to the riskers go the spoils), or with a touch of social engineering (transparency creates fairness for all). When risk rules, it serves to measure how people relate to each other, what they value together, and why they await the future. Not only is the mind to be ordered, but also the body is to be somatized to risk so that what sleeps at night is the knowledge of what can happen by day; a body at rest expresses its own risk capacity. The thicket of ads and images touting finance, the new pedagogies of home economics, the avalanche in regulation and legislation, all point to the medium of risk in which financialization as an imbrication of self in society is to grow. The consciousness of risk that comes from all this diligent socialization could only be confusing as it asks for the normalization of uncertainty and greater and greater tolerance for what proves disruptive. It is a consciousness that invites a drive for reward whose achievement continues to be unsettling.

But much eludes this consciousness, just as rules can scarcely account for the expansive presence of what they try to regulate. Much in the way that people are connected to each other is immeasurable. The cycles of dispossession and ownership brought into being by stockholding and securitization do not themselves engender an awareness of the massive interconnection that has taken place. The reliance on strangers operates unseen for the most part, but it also forces people to come to a reckoning with what they share. The commonality is not readily given by a term like *interest,* which assumes that people know what they need from each other or from a situation before they are able to act together.

The way in which risk distributes association among people is not, by design, directly or immediately accessible. This other socialization of risk shadows the first; it collects all the wealth of society but attaches to no one. One can own shares, but their value is realized only when they depart. Ironically, Marx is usually presumed to have missed this essential part of his analysis of socialization of labor.[41] He is taken to believe that because people are forced into material intercourse, they will necessarily procreate. He did not give himself such an easy charge. Less discussed is Marx's understanding of the socialization of capital, of its own unsettling conditions of movement forcing wealth itself to stand as a social operation and not a personal prerogative of ownership. Risk management in terms of finance is the willingness to let capital decide one's fate but, given this decision, to place that future in the hands of others in the present. Financialization, the elaboration of capital's movement within the integuments of daily life, makes of the future, not an individual's uncertainty, but a present obligation to embrace a risk of what can be made of a promised return.

The future can be seen as feeling the weight or burden of others in the present. This sense of future promotes an awareness that decisions taken by others present one with one's own prospects for what could be, but also a sharing of wealth that is claimed by denying its social form. We can cash out of any given investment, but there is no liquidity on the emerging financial sociality. We have become stuck together in novel ways that generate all manner of discussions over how to rule wealth. Perhaps the most noisy yet elusive speech of this sort was over tax cuts connected to a projected budget surplus in the spring of 2001. The talk itself was dominated by the plunder of the surplus, its decomposition and reallocation to those who already had the most of it. In terms of the first meaning of socialization, these few might be taken as the most deserving; they had risked the most in terms of a tax burden and deserved to get the most back. However pernicious this rhetoric of risk, it could not account for the fact that something had occasioned this public consideration of surplus. Even after the surplus disappeared (as soon as the rebates were made), the attack on it continued in the form of further tax cuts. The other socialization of risk, the collections of capital through the incessant public offerings of the stock market boom, did manufacture this wealth and obliged it to be spoken of as such. Without recognition of this other force of socialization, the only remnant of all that expansion would be lost. But as long as the world continues to be placed at risk, the occasion is likely to return.

4 The New Divisions

A Geography Reconfigured

"There's no place like home," coos Dorothy. This she knows after a tour through exotic lands, where an inscrutable wizard must be unmasked and his powers profaned before normality can be returned. Financialization too has its Oz, which is to be conquered by faith in more righteous principles than had previously ruled. Dot.com millionaires made exciting poster children for the speculative bubble, but for risk management to settle in as a way of life, the abject would need to join the ebullient to give the cautionary tale its power to set things right. The tale itself looks very different depending on who is doing the telling. The poor wicked witch is only trying to secure her inheritance in order to govern her lands. The sorceress may have her corruptions, but should Miss Goody rightfully get the two shoes?

Thus far, the yarn of financialization has been spun as a kind of great cloak that would offer shelter to all. It does not share the universal ambitions of other self-anointed civilizing missions, however unctuous they all may be. This is not to say that Enlightenment aspirations come to a screeching halt the minute the perquisites of finance walk through the door. It is not simply that the reign of finance yields its winners and losers, but it at once justifies why the latter need not be considered while it continues to rely upon the bereft for its success. The specter of very different consequences being brought together within a common space for thinking about them is what geography is all about. The earth trundles along with its eruptions and fissures unfolding across the millennia, but ways of imagining the planet shift at a faster pace. Financialization too augurs a reconfigured geography, certainly not anything utterly new, but some other pressures to place on familiar questions.

Between the Treaty of Westphalia (1648) and the Treaty of Berlin (1885) the globe and its peoples were treated to a practical exercise in universalism; physical territory would be parceled and policed to form nation-states, each with the sovereignty to claim who did and did not belong there (citizenship), and to print money so as to govern universal exchange within national borders.[1] Currency gave face to the wealth of nations and allowed them a means to display their individual integrity and formal equality. This universalism turned out to be rather partisan, as these treaties themselves allowed imperial European powers to set their rule on the rest of the world, divided as it would be between the colonized and the colonizers. The national partitions set the stage for their transcendence in the form of internationalist socialism and decolonizing national liberations, which combined uniquely in revolutionary movements throughout the twentieth century. Universalizing the national territorial form had placed the concept of equality at odds with its practice. Carving the world into nation-states also set in motion twinned geographies, one inside and another external to the nation. The interior geography of the nation-state is expressed in terms of social classes that are formed each in its way as movements of capital and labor etch their social environment. Here the national currency is taken as the prime material for social division.

The geography of nations presumably expressed the disposition of people toward modes of governance, and it reached its apotheosis in the formulation of the Three Worlds, among heads of state meeting at Bandung, Indonesia, in 1955.[2] Both geographies shared a trinitarian design and a difficulty in knowing precisely where the father left the son for the holy ghost. Pointedly, while the idea of the Third World was to express nonalignment with the allied nations of capitalism or socialism, it was some transnational organization that permitted negotiation over terms of alignment. The class trinity offered a bloated middle with which virtually all could identify (if not belong to) that became the means for negotiating the social contract between capital and labor while intending to banish such antagonistic terms from the national imagination.

The two geographies could be readily aligned, as middleness was the developmental equivalent of godliness; the more middle class a nation had, the closer would be the promised land. Middle class is a model of consumption; its bloat requires the growth that present-day inflation fighters find so distasteful. There is no measure by which it is possible to say that the world's peoples are consuming less (though there are plenty of measures to suggest they are more impoverished).[3] A geography is a way of parceling meaning to units so that those units or parts can be neatly summed to a whole that makes each element seem to belong only where it happens to be. The reported crisis of the middle is one of the geography that gave pride of place to the center, not of consumption per se. What was once a stable place from which each person was to build one's own castle in the air, safe from the scrutiny that might declare one's dream foolish, has now been set in motion, placed at risk.

Risk is meant to be as felicitous as consumption once was to give meaning and direction to life, but the self-managed middle turns out to be quite a bit more disorienting. The loss of the privacy that the middle-class "haven in a heartless world" was once based upon is the flip side of the profusion of concern with the private referenced by surveillance technologies and Internet-gleaned information tracking in which the solitude of self is placed at risk. But the attempt to maintain privacy may turn out to be a rearguard effort in relation to the demands for transparency affirmed through the embrace of financial risk. The battle against inflation and on behalf of transparency took place on and contributed to the ruins of what could once be called the Third World. Just as colonialism and imperialism (whose energies I would hasten to say are far from exhausted) oriented the center by what was done to those outside it, so the new global geography of finance crafted its demonstration effect from what it took to be peripheral. Our story should begin there as well.

The Force of Finance

Exporting the idea of progress required quite a sales job and a healthy measure of shrapnel. Spain, Portugal, Britain, France, the Netherlands, Germany, and then the ex-colonial United States took up their civilizing missions, teaching the mother tongue and sport, and building monuments and military bases. As colonies were freed from direct administration, military interventions from former rulers could be called upon to restore order and retain privileged market relations. With finance in the global driver's seat, transnational flows of debt and credit do the steering from afar, but do so by seemingly remote applications of force. People in Granada, Panama, Bosnia, Iraq, and Afghanistan know that the metal still falls out of the skies. Yet whereas imperial expansion lusted for territory it could consider virginal, that which has accompanied the rise of finance has been targeted as much toward exclusion as incorporation. The Gulf War, propagated amid an oil glut, is not over for Iraq ten years hence, and no amount of misery for its people is too high a price to prove the pain of exclusion from the world's advance. For the United States, the Gulf War launched a principle of engagement based on overwhelming force to minimize risk of casualty, an insulation from domestic loss prompted by fear that any body count would erode support for war. Engagement without loss is a slogan fit for the introduction of financialization. The bombing of Belgrade or Panama City in pursuit of criminal suspects Slobodan Milošević or Manuel Noriega couples an idea of justice with wholesale destruction of urban centers. George W. Bush has extended himself a blank check to substitute states for criminals and populations for states in an operation of indefinite retribution he has defined as war. In each case, punishment was meted out to maintain distance where once aid-induced development might have been applied to support interconnection. Directed violence has ever been an instrument of world power, but now punishment has usurped conquest as a rationale as if to remind the unpunished that they must play by the rules or their turn will be next.

Under cover of a domestic war against drugs and crime (and now terror), the carceral capacity expanded in tandem with the booming stock market. The savages and primitives salvaged and saved by colonial attentions proved the project of progress to be big enough to convert, assimilate, and make use of any and all whose path it would cross. Now the premodern has been turned into the antimodern, a panoply of tribes who are lost to reason in their embrace of one kind of fundamentalism or another—religious, national, even musical (as in the case of grunge or raves). The new tribals—whether in Rwanda or Bosnia, or on the streets of Seattle—are the bad objects whose defective culture makes them irredeemable, too risky to enter into any effective calculus for human advancement.[4] These populations are not a surplus held in reserve for burgeoning industrial employment, but expendable masses who may or may not fit within the developmental scheme of a particular nation. The estimate of a billion unemployed worldwide leaves out billions who are not considered part of the world's workforce.[5] It also becomes possible to separate still developing or less developed countries (the seemly and depoliticized term for what the Third World had designated as a force to direct its own course of development), as requiring high rates of growth to meet the insatiable appetites of their wild populations, while mature economies can focus on discipline and containment encouraged by low rates of growth. Growth in economy and in population can readily collide, leaving the latter as damaged goods and therefore unmarketable or in need of rapid liquidation.

Even the permutations in justifying a deployment of the Star Wars missile shield speak to a shift in the logic of violence from the fixed geopolitical territories of mutually assured destruction to a fluid net in which any rogue nation's aeronautical spittle can be kept off the shiny face of the financial party. Whether or not the missile shield could ever be implemented becomes a question that is secondary to its continual reinvocation as a figure of universal exclusion. The extraterritorial aspect of this concept of defense responds to the practical loss or expense of permanent bases around the world with the hubris that territory need no longer be held. The advent of finance has been particularly violent for what had been the Second World, or bloc of socialist nation-states. The million-person-a-year population loss in Russia is but one ripple of what has politely been referred to as a transition. Given that much of Second World productive capacity was suddenly rendered beyond the efficiency of profitability, a massive fire sale made the socialist economies resemble more a very hostile merger and acquisition to extract immediate cash than anything as expansive as an introduction of capitalism.[6] If, however, China has retained some socialist governance, it has done so through expanded manufacturing and limited speculation, the opposite exposure to Russia's. Most paradoxical is Cuba, where the United States has kept itself at speculative bay through the embargo while a parallel dollar economy subsists with the taut net of social benefits.

The new world order of finance was secured in crisis, and in this regard, what others were made to abide was meant to serve as a model for domestic consumption.[7] As finance emerged as a rubric for governance, not only revenue-depleting scarcity (by tax cut and redistribution to corporate needs), but also the new common sense of money management, contained social allocations while tying labor to market vagaries through extending consumer credit. Net wages decline when newly created jobs pay less than the ones they replace. But when currency devaluations are medicine for errant economies, wages are suddenly worth less. Such are the costly cures meted out in Mexico, 1994; Thailand, July 1997; Russia, August 1998; Brazil, January 1999. But to reduce the worth of a currency suddenly presents it in oversupply. This monetary excess capacity engenders industrial merger solutions like the European Monetary Union or the proposed Argentine adoption of the dollar as its official currency. Financial speculation thrives in this gap between so much to lose and to gain, as each of the previously mentioned currency collapses triggered massive monetary flow. The interplay of factors is stated succinctly by William K. Tabb: "Slow growth was ironically the preferred pattern of investors who feared lowered returns from rising inflation. Slower growth was the conscious policy choice for many governments trying to protect their currencies from appreciation and resultant price pressures and loss of international competitiveness."[8]

The officiating narratives to emerge from the 1997 financial debacles of Thailand, Indonesia, Malaysia, and Korea combined cold-war and orientalist tropes to explain why "Asia" had failed to keep up with the promise of globalization. In the annual economic policy document for the United States, President Clinton's council of advisers freed their trade directives from any culpability for what transpired. Accordingly, the East Asian "recipe for success" was to opt for capitalism over state planning and by so doing become "the shining example for the rest of the world." But outward success masked a tragic inner flaw: "Asian governments relied too much on centralized state coordination rather than decentralized market incentives to maintain their progress."[9] In the same paragraph, the report bemoans insufficient state presence in markets that were "poorly supervised and inadequately regulated."

The co-presence of too much and too little state attention is not meant to be a logical error on the part of the authors, but an absence of cool reason from Asian globalizers that might have averted the whole mess. "Crony capitalism" and "relationship-based banking" speak to the hazards that ensue when affect prevails over interests tended at "arms length." Not surprisingly, further foreign ownership of national Asian banks is meant to check such cultural deficits. As with the initial response to the 1930s Great Depression, bankers were first tossed the baton. Only after matters got worse and U.S. investors became afflicted with similar bouts of unreason did U.S.-led versions of increased "centralized state coordination" come into play.

According to Clinton's economists, the precipitates of the Asian contagion were these: "excessive corporate leverage, financial fragility resulting from poorly designed capital market liberalization, foreign indebtedness, a slowdown in export markets, worsening terms of trade, and the development of overcapacity in many sectors" (ERP, 1999, 233). The naive question at this point is, If Asia's sins of irrationality were so abundant, why the rush to invest? Here the orientalist veil descends. The flaws were invisible to even the keenest-eyed investor because financial institutions of the East lack what is called "transparency." Generically speaking, transparency is the "what-you-see-is-what-you-get" (wysiwyg in computer-software speak) of finance. The link between computers and finance is not simply homologous. Synergy is achieved under the banner "Information is control." As policy, transparency is one of the central tenets promulgated by the self-declared guardians of the globe, the G-22. This working group of the most globally active economies, nominally convened by the IMF in the spring of 1998, generated the position papers that would become the IMF's own policy platform for a new financial architecture with itself nominated as the global "lender of last resort."[10]

Technically, the idea of transparency is to merge accountancy techniques with those of economic forecasting. To raise themselves from the depths of opacity, globally aspiring economies are to supplement annual budgeting with multiyear medium-term "frameworks" of financial plan-

ning. The expectation is that forecasting parameters of capital flows (here an acceptable form of state planning) will
lead to predictable stabilities in monetary movements, where
the commitment to low inflation simulates a constant environment throughout the duration of the scheme. Without
inflation to distort the relation between present values and
future prices, information can deliver sanity to the markets.
Beyond the structural adjustments enjoyed by those who
are the targets of inflation fighting, transparency wields a
new disciplinary axe. In the plans of these new architects,
the estimates for the medium-term budget frameworks become contractual hard budget constraints for nations seeking international loans, credits, and underwriting.[11] This new
deal for the indebted was trotted out on November 17, 1998,
by the IMF as the New Arrangements to Borrow (NAB).
Whereas under the *ancien régime* of the 1980s postcolonial
nations had to cut domestic social expenditures in exchange
for new loans, now they must apply increasing self-discipline even to be worthy of consideration for further debt.

The United States was at first reluctant to contribute to
the crisis that its free-trade policies had abetted, claiming
that to do so would only foster what economists call "moral
hazard," the assumption of unmanageable risk on the expectation of salvation. Yet the treasurers and secretaries of
finance soon came to appreciate the cost-effectiveness of
this new insurance policy on U.S. privilege. Of the NAB, the
president's economic councillors chortled, "Through the
IMF, moreover, the United States succeeds in leveraging its
own contributions toward crisis resolution" (ERP, 1999,
249). Because the U.S. contribution is an interest-bearing
claim on the IMF that can be cashed in or liquidated, the
$18 billion ponied up by the United States does not get
treated as an outlay in the federal budget (ERP, 1999, 250).

Leveraged hegemony, the key to globalization's kingdom, requires leveraged participation—making a pinch go a very long way by defining the terms under which contributions combine.

How had risk management turned into its opposite? Bum luck perhaps. Mathematical rapture more likely. The IMF *World Economic Outlook* noted almost coyly that the econometric models used globally provide a "false sense of precision"[12] because the historical data they extrapolate from cannot predict departures from what has happened. The future is betrayed by the past. The report goes on to recommend "a balanced (lack of) respect for statistical models" (59)—shortly after designing a new policy based on forcing transparency on those contagion-stricken nations to the east, arguing that if opacity was the enemy, it lay within. "The argument often heard in the aftermath of the Asian crisis was that no one could see through the opaque financial structures and markets. Yet the markets and institutions that experienced the turbulence this summer [1998] are the most open and transparent in the world. Why then were potential dangers not more accurately perceived at an earlier stage?" (65).

Here is where transparency and risk management tug at each other nastily. The former pertains to budgetary accounts and the latter to transactions off the books. The mathematical models of the financial centers and the close encounters of the Asian contenders add to the same disordering effects. Regulatory mechanisms mushroom, but regulatory control is pushed farther from reach. The Basel Committee on Banking Supervision, the closest thing to a global regulatory body for banks and the "highly leveraged institutions" like Long Term Capital Management that supplement them, recognizes this contradiction. The committee admits that they're not able to define what they are supposed to be regulating and that, if they could, the elusive entity could pick up shop and move "offshore" where their activities would again become invisible.[13] Beyond the prospect of capital flight, leveraging introduces systemic confusion as to who owns what risks because discretion must be maintained so as to avert panic. When parties to contracts are strangers to each other's creditworthiness, logics of accountability cannot be applied.

That the negativities attributed to the other are an internal feature of the colonial self is a discovery only for the IMF. As evidenced in the previous chapter on risk, the related sociological commentary on globalization has for some years insisted that it is a reflexive phenomenon.[14] In light of the recent financial shenanigans, we could add, self-awareness hurts. Irrationality cannot be displaced elsewhere. Now that globalization is inside us and we in it, it becomes possible to speak of its limits. This is not to entertain the pernicious notion that all the world has become the same, joined together through protocols of risk management and transparency into a vast personal responsibility seminar. There does, however, need to be a way to address the unsettling triumph that reigned in the United States until the end of the millennium came crashing down. The indices of victory were legion: high growth rates, low inflation, strong stock markets, budget surpluses, strong business investment rates, more jobs, higher wages. Wealth abounds. Before the bull market was declared dead in March 2001, stocks had increased tenfold since the 1982 recession. Corporate profits doubled between 1991 (the last time there was a glitch in the prosperity train) and 1998 (ERP, 1999, 431). The United States funnels in far more credit from abroad than it metes out (the current account deficit in which the rest of the world subsidizes U.S. expenditure now increasingly goes to private portfolios rather than government bonds) (ERP, 1999, 263). After the confetti had fallen in 2001, recession was a far greater menace in the export-oriented Asian economies, which had been hit a few years earlier, than it was in the United States. More nefarious still, the collapsed Towers twinned the failings of foreign policy and domestic economy that could then be displaced elsewhere. Triumphalism entombed the sense of violation and grief alongside an unaccountable innocence and insularity that had allowed people to believe that such horrors of the world could not happen here.

The Poor Get More

None of the triumph speaks to those left off the bandwagon. In the 1960s expansion, elimination of poverty could be considered a sign of good faith in the universality of progress. Between 1959 and 1973, poverty rates in the United States were cut in half, from 22.4 percent to 11.1 percent. In the great boom of the 1990s the reduction came late and was miserly by comparison. Not until 1999 did poverty fall below what it had been at the peak of the prior business cycle (1989); it rose between 1989 and 1995, and only fell by one percentage point (14.1 to 13.1) in the second half of the 1990s, so that the remarkable 1990s actually had higher rates of poverty than the decade before.[15] Beyond questions of redistribution of wealth, the very shape of how expansion relates to population was being reconfigured.

The more limited vision of what can count as gain is captured by what Andrew Leyshon and Nigel Thrift call "geographies of financial exclusion," "those processes that serve to prevent certain social groups and individuals from gaining access to the financial system."[16] If exclusion is indeed part of the system, then the issue may be less who can gain access than who accesses gain. If a standard risk calculus is applied to the poor, money becomes more expensive for them to borrow because of longer terms for payment, less collateral, and lower future wealth—all determinants of loan risk likely to result in default. Lacking property, poor people are more likely to borrow to supplement wages, to pay medical bills, to make ends meet. Yet the likelihood of assuring a negative outcome is enhanced by exorbitant interest rates. Michael Hudson, who has found inner city check-cashing outlets in the United States charging 2000 percent, has sketched the contours of a "poverty industry" that takes in hundreds of billions of dollars a year. Such a lucrative market is not left to community-based entrepreneurs. Hudson reports, "More and more, the merchants who profit from the disadvantaged are owned or bankrolled by the big names of Wall Street—Ford, Citibank, Nationsbank, Bank-America, American Express, Western Union. Lesser known Wall Street companies are also grabbing a piece of the action. Add up all the businesses that bottom-feed on the 'fringe economy' and you'll come up with a market of $200 to $300 billion a year."[17]

One thing that the large consumer credit houses possess is the means to badger people in default. In practices that eventually led to a class-action lawsuit, the conglomerate ITT had collections agents who called an unemployed woman with a $2,000 loan "and her friends and relatives night and day, at one point demanding that she send them her unemployment benefits."[18] Bad credit forms its own penal colony that, far from disconnecting people from the attentions of finance, renders indebtedness a total institution. Hardship debt burden is pegged at 40 percent of annual income, a distinction that increases as income lessens. In 1998, for example, amid the cornucopia of boom, 2.1 percent of those households with annual incomes of $100,000 or more were in the high-debt-burden category, while for those taking in less than $10,000, 32 percent were so designated.[19] Financial troubles bring intensified relations, however unwanted these may be. Redlining, declined credit, and other forms of exclusion only bring added work and in that regard opportunity for disciplinary contact with financial regimens.

Poverty in this regard is not simply a lack, but an excess of attention, both for those subject to it and for the general morality tales that are to be drawn from those who give up privacy for public demonstration of need. If the universal promises of progress are to be abandoned or renegotiated, the financially excluded cannot be invisible, but must be placed on display through novel approaches to their self-management. What is touted as newfound independence for the poor rests upon different lines of dependency on the assembly of vouchers, credits, and small loans connected to the various programs of reform. This is not to deny the material improvements that may ensue from even the most hard-nosed approaches to disciplining the poor. The logic is that the poor must find their own way and therefore cannot stake a claim on the huge masses of wealth that the financial expansion generated for its own.

The dependency involved is part of the gendering of poverty, and it translates across the seas into the special place of women in the emerging industries of microcredit. This approach to managing poor populations is one more erasure of the boundary between First and Third worlds that can said to be constitutive of the new geography.[20] Without doubt the partition served the constituents differently. The self-designation of Third World was meant to open up more room for development through nonalignment and in that regard was not inconsistent with the universalist aspirations of progress. Since socialist nations outside of Eastern Europe and the Soviet Union could also be part of the Third World, as China and Cuba were, the term could make reference to a postcolonial world where the critique of capitalist imperialism translated into support for various revolutionary movements.

For that intersection of the North and West said to comprise the First World, the distant Third was a source of cheap labor and materials to help subsidize government transfers to citizens who could all count themselves beneficiaries of global inequalities. The emerging global alliance of women that received some organizational attention at the 1995 Beijing Conference on Women speaks to a condition that cuts against the presumption of citizenship-aligned privilege.[21] Certainly it was always true that working people sent to war against each other shared more of life's conditions than those doing the sending, but the belief in the righteousness of the nation and the privileges of citizenship could serve as a palliative.

With financialization's more parsimonious state, the case is tougher to make that the interests are so clearly apart and that, with abandonment of welfare entitlements, sticking with the state is such a good bet for the citizens of the North. It's no wonder that military planners are so concerned about body count when they deploy soldiers in the former Third World. This ultimate equality in death that war makes its opportunity is treated more now as a threat to maintenance of boundaries violated by a change in the domestic social contract. Combat, we are told, remains the preserve of men. That restriction reserves for women the demonstration of what the new entente can yield. While the fully financialized benefit from the powers of anonymous ownership through securitization, poor women are to avail themselves of local powers of face-to-face interaction to acquire the appropriate discipline to lift themselves out of poverty.

One vehicle has been the advent of the village bank, a microfinance institution backed by government, nongovernmental organization (NGO), or private bank. Rather than placing blame for success or failure on a state or development agency, these banks operate through "peer pressure." According to one supportive account, "The Bank—a sort of collective of thirty women—has to be able not only to handle the collection and storage and use of the repayments it receives from members, but to enforce repayment. It can do this by warning bad payers that if they do not repay on time then the next external loan will be delayed, causing inconvenience to all the other members. If the 'shame' of this is not enough to persuade the recalcitrant member to pay up, the group can decide to expel her, or, sometimes, collect the money due by confiscating some of her goods."[22]

The mother of these banks is the Grameen (which means village in Bengali), founded by Bangladeshi economics professor Muhammad Yunus in 1976. Yunus had worked with poor women who made bamboo stools. Lacking collateral and credit, the women became beholden to male traders from whom they borrowed money and to whom they had to sell their goods. Grameen displaced the authority of these men with a hierarchy of men to which the groups of women would report. The premise of the lending is to empower rural women through mutual interdependence and trust. Formally treating the loan centers as if the women were a homogeneous group within the village conflicts with local hierarchies and factions to which women are assigned. The debt arrangements also ignore the links between borrowers and loan officers (who are commonly relatives), and this shift in turn undermines the trust thought to issue from propinquity. Aminur Rahman, an anthropologist who studied these groups, concluded: "The failure in building mutual trust and support with each other in loan centers compels peer loan group borrowers and the bank workers to impose certain forms of repayment discipline—coercion and even debt recycling—that contradict the objectives of generating trust, mutual support, and solidarity. In reality, women borrowers in the loan centers build and maintain factional instead of solidarity groups for their own strategic reasons."[23]

Such findings should give pause to advocates of communitarian solutions to the anomic conditions of the modern world. Rahman goes on to describe what happens when the virtuous cycle of community life turns nasty. "The institutional debt burden on individual households in turn increases tension and anxiety among household members, produces new forms of institutional domination, and increases violence toward many clients of the project" (150). There is no reason to assume that microcredit would have the same consequences everywhere, but at the very least, these findings should introduce more caution than has been the case in assuming that local, interpersonal attachments can circulate as a kind of universal good. While the millions involved in such practices represent an impressive number, far larger are the numbers of subsistence farmers or waged workers left out of the small business assumptions of producing goods for exchange.

The ambitions of microcredit know no bounds. It is intended to be as at home with the poor in Oakland as in Bangalore, and by so doing alter the scale through which poverty becomes part of global finance.[24] In the 1980s, the global poor would fall into that vast trench of the "unbankable," which was how John Reed, then CEO of Citicorp, regarded the four-fifths of the planet's population who were unworthy of his attentions.[25] No longer. While in practice Reed's estimate may still hold, his disinterest does not. In 1997 the first Microcredit Summit was organized with the goal of creating a poverty-free planet by 2025 through the extension of entrepreneurial activity. By 1999 microcredit had been extended to more than 23 million clients, 75 percent of whom were women. According to its annual report, "Experience shows that women are a good credit risk, and that woman-run businesses tend to benefit family members more directly than those run by men."[26]

As the study of Grameen suggests, being a good credit risk may not be good for women. On one hand, far from creating self-sufficiency, the global initiative for microcredit, were it to succeed, might more readily spread experienced dependencies. On the other hand, there is no doubt that the project is being taken seriously by national leaders, like Mexico's own head entrepreneur, president Vicente Fox, who hosted the 2001 Latin American summit in Puebla with a plenary theme of "Working Toward Institutional Financial Self-sufficiency While Maintaining a Commitment to Serving the Poorest Families." Currently, through egrants.org, it is possible to make "donations" to the summit on-line. Can securitization of the poorest be far behind? Under the old geography, citizens of the First World consumed overseas goods made cheap by labor kept at bay by repressive states. The new arrangement indentures women who may risk a beating to maintain their good credit rating for overseas investors. Modernizing development schemes rest upon large-scale infusion of First World industrial products to create urban centers of cheap labor. The financialization of the poor can proceed with comparatively little investment. Bamboo stools can be made without advances in public health or infrastructure, although deforestation of bamboo stands may prove a problem. Such risks would be borne by women as investment opportunities for others, converting debt into what George Caffentzis has called a "productive crisis."[27]

The solution to the pathologies of poverty's high risk can be found in the former Third World. Poverty would enter a new bond-age, where the stigma was traded for low risk.[28] The price of low risk that microcredit advertises is low return. Thus the poorest entrepreneurs may be lifted out of poverty but not into the embrace of the higher returns that finance promised. These contradictions are not lost on the women who are the objects of these schemes.[29] The world summits meant to manage them can become unwitting conduits for the articulation of new critiques and demands, as the financers have found wherever they try to meet, be it Seattle, Washington, Prague, Ottawa, Göteborg, Genoa, or New York. The WTO, IMF, G-8, World Economic Forum (WEF)—the conveners of these various meetings—are not one organization, but they have been melded into a single ruling interest by the protests. What is typically presented as the disruptive antics of a few privileged anarchists from the Ruckus Society needs to be linked more directly to the global conversion of poverty into lines of credit that lead from the villages of Bangladesh to the mobile encampments of the World Bank.

The bank has already signaled its retreat from the large-scale development projects it had helped to underwrite only a few years back, and microcredit speaks to the economics of its embrace of "localization" ("sharing responsibility for raising revenues") as a way forward.[30] Such shared respon-

sibility is supposed to issue from greater cultural understanding of how customs and traditions can be invoked to
involve people in the World Bank's proposals. The celebra-
tions of the local are the refraction in cultural terms of development's own retooling for the world. Far from letting
such institutions off the hook, their meetings instance a
kind of global mediation of the local that they have claimed
to champion. More than rendering public the closed-door
arcana of world finance, the protests reference the instabil-
ity of financializing populism itself. The better organized
and prepared the protestors become, the more extensive the
affiliated groups (the protest for the Genoa meeting in July
2001 listed 700), the more the heads of state seem to take
up the agenda of the streets as their own (debt relief, environmental protection, human and labor rights), even as
they disavow the legitimacy of the protestors. What might
have once been restricted to technical deliberations has now
been elaborated in more ambitious terms.

Though intended to remain local, risk management for
the poor, in practice, circulates globally with unexpected
combinations and political demands all part of the return.
Microfinance is dangled before the global poor so that they
might identify themselves as entrepreneurs and not as la-
borers or part of a surplus population. Credit is easier to dis-
tribute than land, but it has a delocalizing aspect. By lump-
ing the poor together across nations and regions, the World
Bank and the various financial summits that emulate it help
to define a new geographic continuity, a shared space of
risk, that as much organizes certain demands into a chain of
command that leads to their door as it applies self-management to cordon off the spread of needs for development.
Among the nearly 3 billion people living on less than $2 a

day, there is still plenty of room for exclusion, but the presence of so many entrepreneurs around them is somehow supposed to lift their boats as well.

It would be foolish to think that the mere presence of a global space of poverty would wipe out national, regional, or subnational affiliations.[31] Just as globalization has reinforced certain national affinities, so too the nation-state's indifference to incorporating all within its borders tears violently at any conception of homogeneous global space, even of the poor or disfranchised. What financialization of the poor has done is to make poverty something other than lack. It is both a means of gain for others (which it always has been) and a principle of association in its own right (which it has only been spasmodically). The geographic interest of the poor lies in the gap between the concern to eliminate poverty and the dependence upon it. Equally, this interest is torn between its transcendence of any juridical boundary and its complete delineation of persons according to their access to credit and category of risk.

Girdling the Middle

The financialization of daily life turns out not to be for everyone, or more precisely, it becomes the means through which people are measurably different. Before the world's poor broke up the party, socializing ownership seemed to make room for all. Instead, we need to imagine the space that occupies the middle that girdles the globe. By sheer number, those that could count themselves at the midriff of this terrestrial orb have reached unprecedented proportions. The question is whether there is enough in the bulge to center the world's aspirations. If, as suggested in previous chapters, the middle has lost its utopian promise, where does the vision spring from to excite people about the new hegemony of finance? More often than not, hope is laid at the door of technology. Unlike previous incarnations of technological salvation of human need, this one seems poorly equipped to do the job. Many are the approaches to the historical evaluation of technological change. The proliferation of computers that drive financialization have been assessed in terms of the increases in overall productivity that they make possible and in terms of their compression of social time and space. The spread of computers is also credited with foregrounding knowledge and information in industrial production and reconfiguring the relations between culture and nature as the machine's functions become intrinsic to human expressions.[32]

The paradox identified for progress—the more its measures advance, the farther away it appears as an ideal—seems apt for the myriad pronouncements of technological revolution as well. It is possible to track the dissemination of computers or Internet connections globally and evaluate obstacles to access and encroachments on privacy. For example, by dint of personal computer ownership alone, U.S. households possess about a third of the world's total, while almost half of the Internet users reside in North America.[33] China, however, a nation where a fifth of the world's population lives (1.2 billion) had an estimated 40 million personal computers and 7 million Internet users as of late 1999.[34] It is easy to say that all this could change in the next few years, but the question is, How can this difference be assessed? Excluding Japan, in the Asia-Pacific region there is now an Internet user population of almost 13 million who generate nearly three-quarters of a billion dollars worth of exchange. By the year 2004, users are projected at 100 million and revenue estimated to top $87.5 billion.[35] These figures represent dramatic growth, but highly uneven development.

Appraising the subjective state that a new technology calls for, however, is a more daunting exercise. It is not as if the world stands still or produces a singular experience that could be used as a benchmark for future changes. Rather, the claims for what technology is supposed to do to life need to be assessed in their own terms. The power of technology to dazzle, to bewilder, to reveal a future better than the present, rests more on its powers of spectacle than productivity. Whether in advertising, television, or film, computers have flooded the public eye, with a marketing intensity unrivaled for other home appliances. Compared with the telephone, the refrigerator, or the automobile, their dissemination has been more rapid. As a picture of life idealized, the computer has had a tougher time, though not for want of exposure. It seemed that from the 1980s on, few Hollywood movie products were without a computer in one scene or another. Perhaps the redundancy of one screen on another canceled the little one out, but the familiar clacking of keys and cursory movement hardly signify kinetic or dramatic excitement.

If not a revolution, the information reform at its simplest makes two promises: to make communications faster and bring them closer. Speed is calibrated most prosaically with a constant, in this case the eighteen-month turnaround for doubling the power of microprocessors, a marketing strategy elevated to the status of a "law" named for Intel co-founder Gordon Moore. Each generation of Pentium chip has accelerated processing capacity to the point where images can move across the screen at the rate they would on TV. E-mail communication is encumbered more by the speed of typing (or speaking) than by rates of transmission. Even assuming that what people crave is speed, the computer alienates the experience of hurtling through space from the message, and it is more likely to engender frustration at the expectation of instantaneous exchange than to register pleasure of having connected more quickly than previously possible.

Where speed is most germane to financial markets is in the turnaround time for transactions. There is some interval of time between the placement of a stock trade and its actual settlement or payment. In 1995 the industry standard shifted from five days to three. The new initiative, considered the most ambitious to date, is slated for completion by 2004, is called T + 1, and aims to realize a trade within one day. By increasing turnaround time, not only does the rate of accumulation increase, but the risk exposure is diminished. For example, in 2000, roughly $375 billion in trades were outstanding on a daily basis, so that within any three-day cycle, more than $1 trillion was unsettled. At the present rate of expansion of trading volume, exposure would reach nearly $3 trillion by 2004. If a company's share price plummets or there is general market volatility of the sort tied to the Asian or dot.com meltdowns, millions can be burnt in hours, and traders are in for large losses. The T + 1 initiative is intended to synchronize information exchange globally and approach real-time processing of stock transactions.[36] The ability to respond to and profit from risk should increase accordingly. While the sums of money involved are staggering to consider, the speedup is most likely to affect the working conditions of the 772,200 employees of the securities industries (13). They can expect to live volatility in a way that few others can.

In terms of propinquity, interactivity and the intimacy of mediated space would seem to take live interaction as their model rather than their object of transcendence. In an effort to create a sense of brandable permanence amid product volatility, simplicity and user-friendliness are currently the watchwords of web design, not dazzle or extravagance. No longer exotic, the World Wide Web means to become a quotidian workhorse through which corporate logos and identities provide the intimacy that bridges public and private, home and work. The entertainment functions of the Web are pornographic both in content and by formal design (or its absence). The proliferation of pornography was already well under way with the videocassette, and the self-expression of everyday designers and chatters could be considered a kind of libidinal excess that helps to swell the spaces of the private precisely when they are matters of such public interest.

Yet far from progress's ideal of the autonomous individual, this highly meditated self unfolds with an eye ever over the shoulder. The financial correlate is that on-line investment allows you to become more intimate with your money, or more precisely, to live transactions as a kind of intimacy. A recent Morgan-Stanley television ad invites you to "move your money" through corporate affinity. The camera pans a line of men's shoes waiting to be shined until it pauses on an elegant women's pump. The voice-over beckons, "Welcome to the new old boys' club. Less old, less boys." Visually, what starts as a penchant for shoes can allow all to rub shoulders. Corporate comfort this, and not the reminder that you'll have to click to get it. The computer screen's intimacy may aspire to the suspended disbelief of the proscenium theater's fourth wall, which, to create its closeness, must make itself disappear—a spectacle of closeness that erases itself.

None of this minimizes teletechnology's capacity; it only accounts for its failure to impress in the way that would have been expected as its application is advanced. If the far becomes near more readily, the distant future is all the less fantastic. By making hitherto far-flung interaction more intimate, many efficiencies may be realized, but without making much of a spectacle of themselves. Besides telecommunications, computational capacity has been applied to the animation of all manner of machinery and system, from toasters to transit to manufacturing. The whole premise of embedding computers in daily life makes them less visible for being more widely applied. It goes without saying that spectacle is based on visibility and an impassable gulf between viewer and viewed. The achievement of computers is to render their operations invisible to the operator while promising that interactivity means that what you see is what you get.

When generalized to the built environment, the computerized world looks to all appearances starkly like the one it replaced. According to one celebrant, utopia, the projection of an idealized space, has given way to e-topia, which nestles in the ruins of existing urbanity: "In the twenty-first century, then, we can ground the condition of civilized urbanity less upon the accumulation of things and more upon the flow of information, less upon geographic centrality and more upon electronic connectivity, less upon expanding consumption of scarce resources and more upon intelligent management. Increasingly, we will discover that we can adapt existing places to new needs by rewiring hardware, replacing software, and reorganizing network connections rather than demolishing physical structures and building new ones."[37]

This view puts the best possible spin on architecture's present lull in new urban construction, offering fresh esthetic value to interior conversion. But the spectacle of difference that utopia was supposed to provide through the creative destruction of capital's physical centers will apply more to the perpetual excavation of city streets and disembowelment of its buildings than any wholesale aspiration to convert the skyline. Doubtless this is a pronouncement that applies more to New York or Sienna than to Phoenix or Shanghai.

Whether "e" or "u," every topos puts its place of origin on display, wittingly or unwittingly. Whatever its prejudices, this vision of the future is very different from ones of the recent past based on spectacular images of growth and consumption. Critics like Jean Baudrillard made a career of announcing and bemoaning the spectacle. Baudrillard's *Consumer Society,* originally published in 1970, speaks of the "miraculous status of consumption" and the "vicious circle of growth."[38] For Baudrillard, the profusion of objects stands as a spectacle outside the self through which perpetual growth is itself the route to a profaned affluence, a society without myth or history other than that of further consumption itself. Just as the retreat from growth as orienting a market economy has not stopped practical concern that GDP continue to increase annually (only to maintain a slightly lower rate of 2.5 percent rather than 5 percent), so too, the disenchantment with consumerism has done nothing to curtail real consumption.

If the myths of growth and consumption have fallen, it is not so easy to pull the curtain on them and reveal the truths that the wizard wanted to keep secret. Transparency and low rates of inflation are concepts that can be broadly affirmed in measures of public opinion, but this is not as resilient a result as the wholesale production of a mythos. For all the work that financialization demands, even for all the wealth it delivers to its remade middle, it has produced a regimen of discipline without a prescriptive pleasure. Margaret Thatcher, who did as much as anyone to usher in the reign of finance, was fond of saying "There is no alternative" (or TINA). Tiny Tina is now grown up, and still she sees no future in herself.

Though it is intended as such, the abdication of any utopian promise to market life should not be taken as a general attribute of humanity. TINA is self-referential and simply leaves the field wide open for others to enter their accounts. The massive advertising campaign unleashed under "The Fall of Communism" did little to explain what had been or what was to come, but it was certainly meant to get capitalism off the hook of needing to promise any dramatic life transformation. That financialization is decidedly not a utopian project makes plain how the market delivers its wants and amasses wealth with the very open question of what it is for. If the middle was once all about insulated security, a safe perch from which to view a world of possibility, the domestically intrusive labor of self-managed finance is vulnerably exposed in a way that no office of homeland security could remedy.

Financial Visions?

How then are we to think of the wealth that finance has wrought? During the 1990s, records were broken for the longest period of continuous economic expansion and the longest and largest bull market. Besides the vinyl shards of broken records, what is there to show for it? How do we begin to assess the historical significance of this accumulation of wealth? The booms of the 1920s and 1960s were explosive times in many respects, and the 1990s seem tame in comparison, at least in tone (if a decade can sing). The 1920s ushered in consumer society with great fanfare. The 1960s advanced the social economy as a palliative to more radical demands. The 1990s consummation of finance had a certain celibacy about it, given all the excess in our midst. The magnitude of prosperity seemed in inverse proportion to any ambition for what to do with it. Of course the magnitude of the boom is only apparent after the fact, but the fact of living through boom times, so loudly proclaimed in earlier eras, remained muted. Perhaps the most staggering statistic of all is $17 trillion raised in the securities markets during the great boom of the 1990s, which is more than was generated in the prior 200 years. This temporal concentration of wealth inserts it into public memory and popular experience such that its very magnitude stands as an object for all to see—at least, potentially. Something would need to be done to activate the vision.

This conspicuousness of wealth is very different from the conspicuous consumption of a century before, insofar as it appears to be the consequence of a miraculous or virtuous economy and not the virtue of individuals who loom larger than life. Insofar as presentation is concerned, Bill Gates is conspicuous for his ordinariness. Warren Buffett is heralded as the investor's everyman. George Soros has written diatribes against the evils of global capitalism. Since these are the most public figures involved with financializing wealth, the visions associated with each deserve some further attention.

First, it is worth seeing how the trade group for finance, the Securities Industry Association, in its annual "briefing book," speaks, in the most general terms, of the virtue of the wealth it seeks to promote, which we might assume suggests some larger purpose:

Savings and investment fuel capital formation, economic growth, and job creation. Businesses and governments draw from the savings pool to invest in new factories and equipment, develop new technologies, build and repair infrastructure, and train and educate the nation's workforce. This investment, in turn, increases productivity, generates additional economic activity, and boosts employment. Then incomes increase, and improvements in the standard of living occur. The U.S. government can help perpetuate this positive cycle by helping Americans save and invest, which in turn, enlarges the pool of capital available.[39]

As a vision, this one certainly has the benefit of being comprehensive yet succinct. It also mimics, in its own structure of wealth begetting wealth, the virtuous cycle it seeks to promote. While "improvements in the standard of living occur," these too are caught up in the circular movement of wealth whose advance is self-justifying as being more of the same. This process is hardly a recipe for nirvana. Nor is it clear how to exit the merry-go-round. Above all, the endless cycling denies the opportunity to stand back and ask the question "What is all this wealth for?" The unprecedented accumulation would seem to ask for no less, especially when it has become easier to put a price tag on vaccinating the world's population or supplying clean drinking water.

If $17 trillion is thought as a single aggregate of wealth, as money that could be raised for some purpose beyond its parceled distribution into more factories and workers, then a discussion of what futures are possible might look very different. Mutual funds broadly indexed to the whole stock market point in this direction, toward ownership of not just productive capacity, but speculative capacity as well. Although the speculative lacks the spectacular to make of it a vision, such longings to make things whole may produce more ungovernable nostalgia than active intervention. The immediacy of socialized wealth presses the question of what might be done differently into the present, as a function of existing abilities and decisions rather than idealizations of a world freed from the shackles of this one.

By forcing the future into the present, financialization imposes a gargantuan scale onto a framework of management. If poverty can be erased by making everyone an entrepreneur, why can't entrepreneurialism be outed for the cooperation on which it rests, and why can't that cooperation be what is extended by wealth, rather than the other way around? The dull cycle of success that the securities folk commend to us might be successfully broken if the powers to decide how to invest wealth were taken seriously. Up to now, such seriousness has been reserved for the successful. Perhaps it's time to see what they have in mind.

Bill Gates may have been in a better position to speak disinterestedly about the future before Microsoft was brought to court for playing unfairly with competitors in the new economy. His two exercises in futurology, *The Road Ahead* (1995) and *Business @ the Speed of Thought* (1999), are, nonetheless, unabashedly self-promotional. The claims of the earlier book that companies like IBM and Apple "have had an immense amount of our cooperation and support" may ring a bit hollow now.[40] Gates will certainly not be the last businessperson to write himself as the future, and his prognostications, including a high volume of consumer on-line trading (181), look, only six years on, a lot like the present. In this respect, the future is effectively at hand for Gates, and it is a well-functioning marketplace, which he terms "friction-free capitalism," that seamlessly converts information into transactions: "Capitalism, demonstrably the greatest of the constructed economic systems, has in the past decade clearly proved its advantages over the alternative systems. The information highway will magnify those advantages. It will allow those who produce goods to see, a lot more efficiently than ever before, what buyers want, and will allow potential consumers to buy those goods more efficiently. Adam Smith would be pleased. More important, consumers everywhere will enjoy the benefits" (183). While technology may be revolutionary, capitalism is only getting closer to the older model posited by its master. Gates's talent is to be synoptic, not inventive. He transcribes the values of a technology onto business, and of business onto society. "If the 1980s were about quality and the 1990s were about reengineering, then the 2000s will be about velocity."[41] We move from efficiency to speed as an end in itself, just as the new technologies promise. But when the gains of the Web lifestyle are realized, they will become invisible, taken for granted (132). Again, the future is backward looking, a "town square for the global village of tomorrow" (131). In bespeaking the digital age, Gates gives a nod to inequality ("mitigate the challenges such as privacy and haves-vs.-have-not," 414) and democracy ("Citizens in every culture must engage on the social and political impact of digital technology to ensure that the new digital age reflects the society they want to create," 414).

The moment of mitigation and democratic reflection—if "engage on" is to be more than time spent in chat rooms—passes within a few lines. Business makes history, one we should all eagerly await. "As tough and uncertain as the digital world makes it for business—it's evolve rapidly or die—we will all benefit. We're going to get improved products and services, more responsiveness to complaints, lower costs, and more choices. We're going to get better government and social services at substantially less cost" (414).

Faster is more, and more is better. Quantity is quality. This is conventional enough logic for marketing a product, but how well does it sell the future? And what future is it that looks so strikingly familiar? What's good for Microsoft is good for GM, but who else gets to be part of the "we"? So long as the company giveth, all is possible: "If companies empower their employees to solve problems and give them potent tools to do this with, they will always be amazed at how much creativity and initiative will blossom forth" (415). Yes, employers will be amazed at how much money their workers can make for them through schemes to get more labor power out of workers (like reengineering), but just how amazed will the workers be when they are laid off or their stock options turn to powder, or their creativity belongs to someone else? Alas, that's the last line of the book, and from Gates, at least, we may never know.

Gates has claimed the mantle of being the world's richest person, and his insights come from this lofty height. He can also look across the way and see the adjacent peaks, the next tallest of which is his good friend Warren Buffett. Buffett's Berkshire Hathaway is no less iconic to the new economy than is Microsoft. Berkshire's ancestor was a nineteenth-century textile conglomerate, and Hathaway is still a brand of men's shirts. Buffett's investment company focuses on stock purchase and acquisition of other companies —Coca-Cola, newspapers, insurance—with long-term prospects for profitability. He has set a stiff price for a ticket to his ball, with original shares priced at $70,000 per unit in 1998, so as to be selective in the company he keeps.[42] If Gates's "velocity" translates into decreasing the turnover time for transactions, Buffett's simplicity—in the portrayal of his personal demeanor as self-effacing, his adversity to luxury (he lives in the $400,000 house where his children were born), and language (recall his role in authoring SEC plain speak discussed in the preceding chapter)—references an accessible socialization of ownership.

Aside from making money for its investors, Berkshire Hathaway weaves the fabric of capital across various industries, promoting shared ownership over product development (or Gates's mastery of a given market). "Although our form is corporate, our attitude is partnership. . . . We do not view the company itself as the ultimate owner of our business assets but, instead, view the company as a conduit through which our shareholders own the assets" (795). Even his limited partners aren't informed of what they own, preserving the anonymity of investment capital. "I won't tell you what we own because that's distracting" (801). He and his staff research what they consider undervalued companies and use others' money to purchase stock and hold it over a long period. "Stocks are simple. All you do is buy shares in a great business for less than the business is intrinsically worth, with management of the highest integrity and ability. Then you own those shares forever" (801). This is utterly standard public advice and reserves for Buffett's mystique the powers of selection to generate yields consistently higher than the market average.

The less-is-more approach even applies to Buffett's philanthropy, which focuses on population control and has therefore been a staunch supporter of women's reproductive rights, notably a $2 million gift in 1994 to fund clinical trials for mifepristone (RU-486), the abortion pill. As if to explain his own exclusivity, concentrating wealth would seem to rest upon there being fewer people to make a claim upon it. The Buffett Foundation is to be his legacy, a monument to accumulation meant to be the world's largest charitable organization at his death. Buffett is adored for his mastery of trenchant aphorism, and most of what he has to say, unsurprisingly, pertains to making money. He fits well the picture of the Protestant ascetic who answers to a calling: "Money is a by-product of something I do extremely well" (799). For the presentism of the investor's mind repeated for the long term, the future will have to wait. Money is not even an end in itself but simply a measure of performance. From this perspective, ownership can be amalgamated and wealth amassed, but the larger purposes of the endeavor as constituting any kind of societal project are difficult to grasp.

If Buffett offers little insight into what capitalism is for, George Soros might be considered its self-anointed philosopher-king. Buffett is a master technician, history's greatest stock picker. Soros, whose money is made in speculation and arbitrage, wants the world to listen to him, and his many books and the Soros Foundation are devoted to that end. Soros is not short on visions of global transformation, for he takes the characteristics of the financial markets to be isomorphic with history as such—and he proposes a theory to explain both. He also sees his speculative activity as testing his ideas about history. In *The Alchemy of Finance* (1987), he argued that there is a reflexive relation between investor bias (thinking) and economic fundamentals (reality) that animates the markets.[43] In *Underwriting Democracy* (1991), he uses the idea from chaos theory of "far-from-equilibrium conditions," used to describe the physics at the origin of the universe, to counter the notion that conditions in any given environment tend toward equilibrium. He then distinguishes three permutations of equilibrium: "dynamic equilibrium (open society); static disequilibrium (closed society); or dynamic disequilibrium (revolution or the boom-bust pattern familiar from financial markets)."[44] As historical referents, open and closed are cold war terms for West and

East, and Soros deploys them according to ideological convention. As an ideal, an open society is one "determined entirely by the decisions of its members" (204).

While Soros would be loath to admit it, such a definition would be at home in many socialist writings, although for him "decisions" refers to the kinds of contractually regulated choices one finds in market transactions taken by individuals. That a state of static disequilibrium could suddenly become dynamic may cast doubt on how static it was in the first place. Indeed, Soros's grand trinity would soon have to devolve to its third, chaotic turn as a general condition, as dynamics become increasingly destructive. A Hungarian émigré to the West in the 1950s who gave up his passion for philosophy to pursue economics, Soros assumes that his accumulated wealth is a principal historical agency that abets revolution, by which he means the Soviet demise. He intends his foundations to use their goal of creating an open society as a "comparative advantage, which we can exploit" (128).

Soros is here pioneering venture philanthropy, which, rather than supporting existing institutions or projects, becomes the chief mechanism for the aims it seeks to effect. Although these ventures operate as nonprofits, they intend change to be won through competition and exploitation of circumstances just as fully as beating the market. "My original objective has been attained: the communist system is well and truly dead. My new objective is the establishment of an open society in its stead. That will be much harder to accomplish. Construction is always more laborious than destruction and much less fun" (128). At the time, Soros seems unconcerned with the human costs of the destruction he is helping to wreak, so sure is he that those who will enjoy the choices and alternatives in the East outweigh those who have lost theirs. At least he is having fun. On Soros's agenda at the time (and later) was to marshal aid from the West to absorb the Soviet alliance. This approach would have demanded reflection on how the surplus wealth of capitalism might best be deployed. Looking back, Soros pines, "the West did not believe in open society as a universal idea."[45] One could add, looking at those in the West left out of the rush to choose, that it did not hold this belief even for itself.

The failed openness of the West does not dim Soros's faith. While he decries the market fundamentalism of a Thatcher or Bush that led the West to lose Russia, he also would have profited handsomely had foreign aid helped make viable his $2 billion acquisition in 1997 of Svyazinvest, the telecom holding company. At the time, he "felt that Russia needed foreign investment more than philanthropy" (245). The more disequilibrium reigned in global finance as in 1997 and 1999, the more Soros advocated comprehensive regulatory approaches, like an international central bank. As the risk on his positions subsided, he could retreat on these ideas for new financial and political architectures as "far too radical" (276–77). Nonetheless, at a time when the financializers are treated as the few individuals entitled to speak for the many, he insists on an internationalist perspective that would increase foreign aid and strengthen institutional frameworks. He envisions a partnership between investment-interested civil society groups like his own and government initiative, led by a United States that could "recognize our fallibility" and "participate in forming rules by which we are willing to abide" (356). While all this was written before George W. Bush came to office, the antipathy with which U.S. foreign policy now regards the world makes Soros's remarks seem far too radical once again. At some point we might expect more to be made out of the antinomy between the Bush regime's promotion of venture philanthropy to usurp government functions and the ungovernable demands of the premier instance of this type.

When philanthropy ventures outside official foreign policy or stands in for popular opinion, it comes close to the ideal of civil society (a sphere of activity independent of state or market) that it wants people to believe in. But if civil society requires the kindness of private wealth, its public freedom is rather tightly tethered to personal interests. The new philanthropy, like microfinance, has no burden to be universal in its reach, but this fact only underscores the social limits to the visions of the future that finance yields. At the same time, something remains unsettling in the confidence that the personal accrual of wealth can solve the world's problems. However worthy, the expenditures of a Gates or Buffett appear remarkably unambitious in scope compared to a Rockefeller, Ford, or Carnegie. Soros is a bit different. If Soros is to be taken at his word, it was finance itself that led him to support revolution. One can certainly argue about which revolution to support and what kinds of global institutionality would be most useful to implement, but what is most salient is how the engagements with global finance open different routes out of the cold war morass by posing the question of what to do with the world's wealth and its capacity to design itself.

Waiting for philanthropy to come is hardly a prudent strategy for those in need of financial support. The idea that only the rich have access to surplus wealth is revised by acolytes of human capital. Human capital takes the model of accumulated wealth and claims that anyone can be valued for what each person has or could amass over time. It makes of the self a portfolio. When the concept is to be illustrated, artists are the favorite examples. Picasso tosses out a sketch in minutes but values it in the years it took him to acquire the ability. David Bowie issued fifteen-year bonds for $55 million against future royalties and concert revenues.[46] The Bowie bonds were held by Prudential Insurance of America. Were they to be securitized and traded, Bowie would become the first fully financialized self. It is convenient for the models of human capital that the exemplars already possess substantial capital of the conventional sort.

One economist, Robert Schiller, did actually propose futures markets for more familiar categories of labor, as a way of ameliorating inequality by giving people access to the amalgamated value of their lifetime earnings:

> By making it possible to hedge the capital value of a stream of aggregate income, perpetual claims or perpetual futures markets, long-term swap markets, or retail analogues of these would facilitate management of the kind of longer-run income risk that really matters to individuals and organizations. Nations or other groupings of people could use such markets to insure themselves against the prospect of a declining standard of living, against the prospect of relative poverty. By hedging such risks, these macro markets would allow the natural tendency for convergence of incomes to reduce inequality of incomes, by removing the shocks that disperse incomes. Thus, the establishment of such markets might make significant progress, in the long run, toward equalizing wealth across nations, regions, and categories of people and, consequently, across individuals themselves.[47]

Whether or not we are likely to ever encounter the nature that allows incomes to converge (or achieve equilibrium) or to create the political entity that would underwrite these markets, Schiller is drawing out a salient implication of taking the financialized self seriously.

Just as securitization presented the specter of replacing individually held property with social property and treating

pooled finance as wealth for any purpose available on demand (liquidity), a securitized incomes market presents labor's futures in a new key. Pooling the potential income of
all who labor and treating it as a force in common makes explicit the interdependencies of those who generate value
upon each other. All would be invested in these labor markets and presumably trade upon the fortunes and misfor-
tunes that others incurred. An individual's labor would be
bonded to others in a manner that would make it difficult
to speak of that person's fate, interest, activity, creativity, or
expansion as a thing unto itself. If the artist once stood to advertise the romantic view of the self-contained and generating individual, the same figure is deployed to advertise the
individual's replacement. Old Peter Drucker got quite nervous at the thought of workers holding pensions and effectively owning corporations. Extending this ownership to labor's collective capacity in itself would no doubt send him
into orbit.

While many variants of shareholder and stakeholder
value take up the socialization of ownership through various forms of securitization, their most typical impulse is to
equate ownership with personalization. Illustrative here is
Jeff Gates's *Ownership Solution*, which offers a communitarian spirituality of personal responsibility "to evoke a breakthrough to a capitalism that fosters a more mindful living."[48]
As in the Grameen bank example, the moral commitments
of local control that assure a "community without communism" can, through their intolerance, exclusions, and invo-
cations of selected traditions, narrow our imagination of the
politics that are available to us.

In light of the rush to propose a final solution, it may be
more useful to insist that the political and organizational expressions of the financialization of labor have yet to assert

themselves. Were they to do so, access to how to think about wealth produced and held in common would expand dramatically. Making everyone a capitalist, entrepreneur, or risk manager assumes that what can be generalized is the exploitation of each over all, that the wealthy individual is the model of success that all should emulate. If both labor and capital are socialized to the point where we are forced to confront them as funds for more profound mutual engagement, then we can draw upon the intricacy of interaction that greatly opens up who and what we can be for one another. The values attributed to capital, to technologies, to wealth, could then rightfully be posed as questions for the future that we want in the present. This reversal of fortune would draw upon finance's means without embracing its ends, engendering a state of immeasurable risk, a departure from expectations whose rewards bear no price.

Summing Up

Any conclusion to the financialization of daily life would, necessarily, be speculative. Increased risk tolerance means greater indeterminacy for what may come. The great crystal ball of prognostication was shattered when progress hit the rocks of its realization. Rather than assuming that all is lost when the future loses its clarity, it should be possible to give some coherence to the rather ungainly phenomenon under consideration here. Synoptically, four overlapping conceptual arenas can be identified: the conjunctural or historical; the geographic or hegemonic; selfhood; and temporality. Not to be too unholy, but financialization is a way of rethinking the trinitarian approach to the social sciences that would partition culture, economics, and politics. The language of economics and concern with its movements have entered daily experience and political considerations to such a degree that it is difficult to say where the three terms part company.

At once regulatory, productive, and experiential, financialization's secrets will have to be mined with other analytic tools. Just to keep the numbers going, the other great divide for thinking about the social world is the dualism of micro and macro. Confusedly a distinction of size and scale of social interaction, it is better approximated as the difference between process and structure. In either case, financialization would remove the bar between the two terms, making global movements of finance intimate with daily life and animating the rules that order human affairs.

Before rehearsing these four areas, a large caveat is in order. It is tempting when identifying an emerging phenomenon to treat it as the only one under the sun, or as replacing all others. As a consequence, the new times seem oddly cut off from the old, and those working under different rubrics or frameworks are cast as irrelevant or out of step. Announcing something new can be a rather divisive business, as well as a reductive one. Whatever financialization is, however extensive its reach, it is not the only historical tendency or way of understanding the present. The demands it makes on people's attentions will be mixed with others. The combinations will no doubt prove volatile. If financialization is not exclusive, neither is it unitary. It divides as much as it unites, sorts as much as it subjects. Too much credit given to finance makes its powers appear unassailable and nonnegotiable—precisely the opposite of what a critical appraisal is meant to do. Doubtless it would take some fancy calculus to integrate all the aspects of financialization. For now, some simple addition will have to do to sum up.

Finance rears its head every time capitalism gets the shakes or undergoes a significant historical turn. At the same time, its control center shifts from the Netherlands in the seventeenth century to Britain in the nineteenth, and lately, the United States. For three decades after World War II when the dollar backed international currency exchange and U.S. military bases jacketed the globe, the U.S. hold on marketable economies seemed absolute. With the unraveling of Bretton Woods in the 1970s, the United States ceded currency sovereignty and wealth share. In 1970 it held two-thirds of the worth of the world's capital markets and a quarter of global gross domestic product; thirty years later these proportions were down to one-half and one-fifth, respectively.[49]

Financialization is animated by the freeing of capital from its prior places of residence, and it is in the frenzied movement of currencies and other instruments of exchange that the mass of money available as investment outstrips the amount invested in industrial capacity. Through stock markets and their ilk, money seems to be made out of thin air (and to disappear back into the same ether), but the social effects of this accelerating circulation are quite tangible. Most saliently, the creation of new wealth forges the medium through which capital and risk are socialized, in which ownership is detached from individuals and assigned to far-flung nets of investors. The proximate effect of this process is to concentrate wealth and the authority to dispose of it in a corporate stratum that lives by finance. At the same time, however, financial self-management becomes a general feature of life for millions linked indirectly through their investments, in turn enlarging the scale of capital.

This expansion of finance comes with a shift in orientation for managing national economies; no longer is maximizing growth the key recipe for prosperity. Just as the material entailments of progress hove into view for the bulk of the world's population, the lights on the stage of universal

human advance dimmed. While the newest wave of enclo-
sures send people flowing into burgeoning global cities, the
great doors of development are closing. All this is the seamy
side of globalization. Statistics can still show improvement,
but the new math doesn't allow the numbers to add up the
way the old arithmetic did. Where growth and progress once
reigned, inflation and transparency are now the watchwords to measure the human condition. The two couplets
are different in meaning but similar in function.

In the name of progress the metropolitan center could
exploit the wealth of the periphery as its own. Lack of transparency outside the West could account for the inscrutable
treatment (under pain of further meltdown) such places received from lending agencies operating for rich nations internationally. If progress is a hopeful vision of the future,
transparency lays the future bare in the present so that further discipline can be applied. While negative growth is associated with failure, hot-wired expansion is inflationary
and therefore unsupportable. The state of nature that required growth silently slipped into an intolerance toward
inflation as its principal law. Growth demands constant vigilance and is nothing to celebrate by itself. It's no wonder
that the record-breaking expansion was nonexpansive and
that material improvements (where they occurred) did not
translate into reported satisfactions. Fighting inflation and
making oneself transparent leave a rather naked truth in
their wake. That civilization breeds discontent is an old yarn.
It remains to be seen whether discontent at the loss of a
myth of growth and progress proves more disruptive than
civilization can bear.

Shifting the fable of humanity's march from progress to
finance invites different ways in which those not directly in
command of social wealth can imagine that there is room for

them too. Participation by the many in a particular way of life arranged for the benefit of the few is a simple definition of hegemony. Financialization aspires to such elegance. The power of the United States is historically unrivaled, yet the consequences of its dominance are far from certain. It's hard to imagine a singular world power seeming so parochial as to leave itself out of a major international treaty, as the United States did in the ratification of the Kyoto protocols on climate control signed by 178 nations in July 2001. The United States gives a smaller share of its GDP to foreign aid than any of its peers, is wayward in its support for the UN, and wants to negotiate down its contribution to other international agencies. The practice of leveraged hegemony intends to give less to get more, both at home and abroad.

The national state is as selective in its international participation as it is in what it offers its citizens to win their hearts and minds. Never relatively generous on social entitlements, the new contract is a do-it-your-selfer. The greatest beneficiaries of government entitlements were not the poor, but corporate interests and college-educated homeowners, the latter forming the baby-boomed middle class once so thoroughly supported by public expenditure. Again, if we were simply talking about indicators, all would be dandy, with unparalleled home-ownership rates and college admissions. Neither is the blank screen on which to project a future of consumer delight and enlightenment that once gave the American dream its legs. Financial self-management leaves no corner of the home untouched. Cradle to grave, dawn to dusk, the *oikos* of economics returns to its original residence where home organizes both labor and its reproduction. By their own reports, people are busier than they have ever been, but business does not translate readily into participation. There remains a yawning gap between the socialized ownership of property that securitization has offered up, and either the dreamscape or the political mobilization appropriate to such expanding interconnections.

The redefinition of the family home as an object of speculation and credit, together with the infusion of its interior design with financial tastes, displaces domestic life in a number of ways. When the home stood for a sturdy separation of private life from public affairs, a good deal of violence could be swept under the carpet of patriarchal authority so as to retain the ordered tranquility. When the family too is transparent, run like a corporate boardroom with full disclosure, authority lies in the marketplace that bisects the domestic economy into a holy writ of allowance (to teach financial literacy) and unpaid chores. The home is no longer an entertainment center, but a medium of age-appropriate financial management whose authority may try to insist that father knows best, but he has to show the math. There is no telling where the skepticism of expertise may stop once all are required to do the research and not assume that delegating authority will yield the highest return.

The financialized self embraces risk. But risk tolerance blends reason into affect. Just as the home is being fully rationalized for investment decision, all the information gathered there is somatized into what sleeping bodies can bear. At the same time, all these decisions are made through others, most typically strangers who reveal themselves in chat rooms or remain the anonymous holders of various securities. The socialization of ownership disperses the self around the world, tying its fate with the most general movements of money. All finance is advertised on the basis of individual gain, but its means are wholly deindividualizing. The individual is more fully one with the vast interdependencies of society than ever before, and the local more fully consequent to the global.

And if all this were not enough on which to stake a claim for the meaning of a term, financialization reorients our sense of time to beckon the future in the present. The banal version of a deflated future is that controlling inflation makes financial investment attractive and simulates a situation where the environment for decision stays the same so as to engender faith in certain lines of reason. Risk management is an orientation toward the future in the present, as calculations of departures from expectation convert events that have yet to take place into measurements of the moment. Advocacy of risk trades its association with danger for one of reward. In practice, those who already have capital to speculate with are most richly rewarded. As a more general conception, viewing the future from the perspective of quantifiable gain takes a lot of the mystery out of what may come. Expectations may fail to materialize, and losses may be incurred, but the parameters of loss and the appropriate responses could themselves be anticipated through any number of hedge maneuvers. Aside from the lucky ones able to make it into the winner's circle, it's easy to dismiss financialization for its baleful effects and absence of vision. No history, no dreams, success made insecure at each moment, all make for an anxious present. The anxiety is very much at odds with the serenity attached to the older dreamscape which only asked that people plug away, consume, and save to achieve a brighter day. Now that all the tools to make the future are to hand, the powers of decision know no bounds. In the absence of spectacular vision, it may be possible to sense more directly how we rely on one another without having to touch.

The feeling that emerges may be that of nothing less than society itself. If so, financialization will have truly delivered the unexpected. A demand on the present that it make use of all the wealth that can be marshaled points beyond the market madness, but does so here and now. Capital dispossesses labor of private life in order to expand unpaid labor in what amounts to a combination of expanded demand and realization of value. Labor, in turn, gets a new kind of association, realized now as a claim on capital itself. This development raises the question of a social surplus not just as an aggregate of wealth, but as an organizational capacity beyond what is needed to make society as it is. This latter capacity should carry with it a return of interest in the promise of active political intervention, as an elaboration of how people might join one another. This activisim would add to the issues of redistribution posed by the present movements grouped under the rubric of antiglobalization, a claim on the basis for social life itself as a function of the meaning of what is done with the wealth made together.

Notes

Unless otherwise indicated, all web sites verified to be accurate as of July 2002.

Introduction

1. *New York Times,* July 27, 1999, p. A7.

2. The fragility of Internet-based banking of this sort is described by Orla Okapos, "Net Banks: More Dream Than Reality," *US Banker Magazine,* February 2000. Electronic version at www.findarticles.com.

3. Information on Wingspan was found on-line at http://home. wingspanbank.com/wingspan/about/about_iboard.htm (1/2000).

4. Joe Sponholz, head of Chase.com, quoted in "Online Banking," *The Economist,* December 4, 1999, pp. 21–23, p. 23.

5. Ibid., p. 22.

Chapter I

1. See World Bank, *Entering the 21st Century: World Bank Development Report, 1999/2000* (New York: Oxford University Press, 2000), p. 14. For a critical analysis of these trends, see Michael Chossudovsky, *The Globalisation of Poverty: Impacts of IMF and World Bank Reforms* (New York: Zed Press, 1998). In the draft of its 2003 World Development report, "Sustainable Development in a Dynamic Economy," the estimate is that 2.5 to 3 billion people live on less than $2 per day. Available on-line at http://econ. worldbank.org/files/13551_04AprRoadMapWEB.pdf (2/02).

2. While there is great contention over how to measure income distribution, standards of living, and relative and absolute poverty, these trends are tracked most comprehensively in a serial put out by Lawrence Mishel, Jared Bernstein, and John Schmitt, *The State of Working America, 2000/2001* (Ithaca, NY: Cornell University Press, 2001).

3. Family income for the poorest fifth of the population rose at a 2.7 percent annual rate, in contrast with a rate of 2.4 percent for the wealthiest fifth of families. Council of Economic Advisers, *Economic Report of the President* (Washington DC: Government Printing Office, 2000), p. 27.

4. Juliet Schor, *The Overspent American: Upscaling, Downshifting, and the New Consumer* (New York: Basic Books, 1998), p. 14.

5. Everett Carll Ladd and Karlyn H. Bowman, *Attitudes Toward Inequality* (Washington, DC: American Enterprise Institute Press, 1998).

6. For discussion of Fordism and post-Fordism as particular logics of wealth creation or regimes of accumulation that engender certain patterns of social life or reproduction, see Michel Aglietta, *A Theory of Capitalist Regulation: The U.S. Experience* (London: Verso, 1979); Stuart Hall and Martin Jacques, *New Times: The Changing Face of Politics in the 1990s* (London: Verso, 1990); Ash Amin, ed., *Post-Fordism: A Reader* (Cambridge: Blackwell, 1994).

7. Data on home ownership can be found at the web site of the U.S. Census Bureau: The Official Statistics, Housing Vacancies and Home-ownership, http://www.census.gov/ftp/pub/hhes/www/housing.

8. W. Michael Cox and Richard Alm, *Myths of Rich and Poor: Why We're Better Off Than We Think* (New York: Basic Books, 1994). Between 1984 and 1994 poor households' ownership of microwaves increased from 12.5 percent to 60 percent and VCRs from 3.4 percent to 59.7 percent. During the same time, these households' ownership of personal computers increased from 2.9 percent to 7.4 percent—as compared to 41 percent of all households (p. 14).

9. Brian Goff, *Regulation and Macroeconomic Performance* (Boston: Kluwer Academic, 1996).

10. For accounts of the emerging regulatory regimes, see Cynthia Glassman, James L. Pierce, Roberta S. Karmel, and John J. La Falce, *Regulating the New Financial Services Industry* (Washington, DC: Center for National Policy Press, 1988), and Clifford E. Kirsch, ed., *The Financial Services Revolution: Understanding the Changing Role of Banks, Mutual Funds, and Insurance Companies* (Chicago: Irwin Professional Publishing, 1997).

11. Robert Guttmann, *How Credit Money Shapes the U.S. Economy* (Armonk, NY: M. E. Sharpe, 1994).

12. An informative account of the rise of bondholding as a dominant interest of speculative wealth is E. Ray Canterbery, *Wall Street Capitalism: The Theory of the Bondholding Class* (Singapore: World Scientific, 2000); pp. 178 and 251 contain the information cited here.

13. Ibid., p. 218.

14. Ibid., pp. 176–81.

15. See David B. Sicilia, *The Greenspan Effect: Words That Move the World's Markets* (New York: McGraw-Hill, 2000).

16. This fact is well documented by Michael Meeropol in *Surrender: How the Clinton Administration Completed the Reagan Revolution* (Ann Arbor: University of Michigan Press, 1998). Meeropol considers the "final sur-

render" of Clinton to be the promise to balance the budget by 2002 and, writing in the late 1990s, considers it "inconceivable" that recession would not occur before that time (p. 262) and that increased rates of growth and productivity would never materialize. That all of these things did transpire within the subsequent years and recession was deferred until Clinton left office should introduce a cautionary note to predictions, even those informed by the most stalwart of critical analysis.

17. Barry Bluestone and Bennett Harrison, *Growing Prosperity: The Battle for Growth with Equity in the Twenty-First Century* (Boston: Houghton Mifflin, 2000), p. 240.

18. Allen Schick, *The Federal Budget: Politics, Policy, Process,* rev. ed. (Washington, DC: Brookings Institution, 2000), p. 30.

19. These numbers were compiled by Theresa Smalec from the government legislative database, http://thomas.loc.gov. They are only a very rough measure based upon using "finance" as a search term. It would seem that the differences are dramatic enough to admit a trend.

20. David Lenhardt, "In Layoff Plans, Reality Is Often Less Severe in the U.S.," *New York Times,* February 19, 2001, pp. 1 and 12.

21. David S. Evans and Richard Schmalense, *Paying with Plastic: The Digital Revolution in Buying and Borrowing* (Cambridge, MA: MIT Press, 1999), pp. 1–2 and 15.

22. Louis Uchitelle, "Equity Shrivels as Homeowners Borrow and Buy," *New York Times,* January 19, 2001, pp. A1 and C2.

23. The perils of the debt load on the status of middle-class life are analyzed with precision in a study by Teresa A. Sullivan, Elizabeth Warren, and Jay Lawrence, *The Fragile Middle Class: Americans in Debt* (New Haven, CT: Yale University Press, 2000), figures taken from pp. 224 and 211, respectively.

24. This was an argument made during days of higher inflation in the 1970s by David Caplovitz, in his *Making Ends Meet: How Families Cope with Inflation and Recession* (Beverly Hills, CA: Sage, 1979), p. 184.

25. Ibid., pp. 3 and 238, respectively.

26. Between 1995 and 1998 the proportion of families owing more than 40 percent of their income in debt payments increased from 13.6 percent to 14.5 percent. *Report of the Council of Economic Advisers, 2001* (Washington, DC: Government Printing Office, 2001), p. 58.

27. Ibid., p. 21.

28. See Robert J. Shiller, *Irrational Exuberance* (Princeton, NJ: Princeton University Press, 2000).

29. Robert M. Collins, *More: The Politics of Economic Growth in Postwar America* (New York: Oxford University Press, 2000), p. 232.

30. Katherine Newman, *Falling from Grace: The Experience of Downward Mobility in the American Middle Class* (New York: Free Press, 1988); William P. Kreml, *America's Middle Class: From Subsidy to Abandonment* (Durham, NC: Carolina Academic Press, 1997); Allison Zippay, *From Middle Income to Poor: Downward Mobility Among Displaced Steelworkers* (New York: Praeger, 1991); Val Burris, *Crisis of the New Middle Class* (New York: Praeger, 1997); Wallace C. Peterson and Frederick R. Strobel, *The Coming Class War: Power, Conflict and the Consequences of Middle Class Decline* (Armonk, NY: M. E. Sharpe, 1997); Robert C. Yeager, *Losing It: The Economic Fall of the Middle Class* (New York: McGraw-Hill, 1980); Alice Coner-Edwards and Jeanne Spurlock, eds., *Black Families in Crisis: The Middle Class* (New York: Brunner/Mazel, 1988); John Oliver Wilson, *After Affluence: Resolving the Middle-Class Crisis* (San Francisco: Harper and Row, 1980); Donald L. Bartlett and James B. Steele, *America: Who Stole the Dream?* (New York: Andrews and McNeel, 1996).

31. Michael J. Mandel, *The High Risk Society: Peril and Promise in the New Economy* (New York: Random House, 1996), p. 8.

32. Ibid., p. 58.

33. Both quotes are from Stan Davis and Christopher Meyer, *Blur: The Speed of Change in the Connected Economy* (New York: Warner Books, 1999), p. 149.

34. Robert Wuthnow, *Poor Richard's Principle: Recovering the American Dream Through the Moral Dimension of Work, Business, and Money* (Princeton, NJ: Princeton University Press, 1996), p. 137.

35. This observation is made by Andrew Hacker in *Money: Who Has How Much and Why* (New York: Scribner, 1997), p. 28.

36. Georg Simmel, *The Philosophy of Money* (Boston: Routledge and Kegan Paul, 1978), p. 470.

37. Robert Frank, *Luxury Fever: Why Money Fails to Satisfy in an Era of Success* (New York: Free Press, 1999), pp. 112 and 73, respectively.

38. Robert E. Lane, *The Loss of Happiness in Market Democracies* (New Haven, CT: Yale University Press, 2000), p. 3.

39. Brian Goff and Arthur A. Fleisher III, *Spoiled Rotten: Affluence, Anxiety, and Social Decay in America* (Boulder, CO: Westview Press, 1999), pp. 49–63.

40. W. Michael Cox and Richard Alm, *Myths of Rich and Poor: Why We're Better Off Than We Think* (New York: Basic Books, 1999), p. xiv.

41. Richard T. Gill, *Posterity Lost: Progress, Ideology and the Decline of the American Family* (Lanham, MD: Rowman and Littlefield, 1997), pp. 171–87.

42. Juliet Schor, *The Overworked American: The Unexpected Decline of Leisure* (New York: Basic Books, 1991), p. 167.

43. Schor, *The Overspent American*, p. 12.

44. A dialogue among these various positions can be found in Juliet Schor, *Do Americans Shop Too Much?* (Boston: Beacon Press, 2000). The statement cited here appears on p. 97. Another account of inflated expectations generating deflations in satisfactions is Frank Levy, *The New Dollars and Dreams* (New York: Russell Sage, 1998). Levy provides the example of late 1980s college educations failing to deliver "good jobs." The result is increasing pressures on youth to improve their vitae so as to gain admissions to elite colleges, p. 89.

45. John P. Robinson and Geoffrey Godbey, *Time for Life: The Surprising Ways Americans Use Their Time* (University Park: Pennsylvania State University Press, 1997), p. 317. Robinson has been involved in time diary studies since the 1960s and has published extensively both alone and with others. I will therefore refer to him alone in the text even when making reference to this particular study.

46. These findings are summarized by Robert Putnam in a preface to the book, Ibid., pp. xv–xxvii. Putnam's own data-driven ruminations on civic life gone to pot can be found in his *Bowling Alone: The Collapse and Revival of American Community* (New York: Simon & Schuster, 2000). Television is a major culprit of malaise for Putnam, especially his reported intergenerational decline in community-mindedness. For Schor as well, TV is the culprit for escalating consumption standards, *The Overspent American*, p. 80.

47. This view is consistent with a range of perspectives on the social construction of time. See, for example, John Bender and David E. Wellbery, eds., *Chronotypes: The Construction of Time* (Stanford, CA: Stanford University Press, 1991); Barbara Adam, *Timewatch: The Social Analysis of Time* (Cambridge, UK: Polity Press, 1995); Carol J. Greenhouse, *A Moment's Notice: Time Politics Across Cultures* (Ithaca, NY: Cornell University Press, 1996).

48. Robinson and Godbey, *Time for Life*, p. 15.

49. This point is made with reference to an allusion to a different conception of physical life based upon chaos theory and particle physics. See Jame Gleick, *Faster: The Acceleration of Just About Everything* (New York: Vintage, 1999), p. 167.

50. Robinson and Godbey, *Time for Life*, p. 56.

51. These data were taken from a Hearst-commissioned Roper Starch poll released January 4, 2000. Leisure hours are reported to have declined from 38.2 in 1993 to 35.3 in 1998. An added 10 percent of respondents concurred that the American Dream is easier to obtain now than so reported in 1993. http://www.roper.com/news/content/news169.htm (1/01).

52. Sixty-two percent in each case. This is a Roper Starch poll commissioned by Circles, a "personal services" provider. http://www.roper.com/news/content/news208.htm (1/01).

53. These figures and estimates are provided by Kirk Kazanjian in *Wizards of Wall Street* (New York: New York Institute of Finance, 2000), pp. 1–2.

54. Joey Anuff and Gary Wolf, *Dumb Money: Adventures of a Day Trader* (New York: Random House, 2000), p. xvii.

55. Ibid., p. xvi.

56. Ibid., p. 4.

57. Ibid., p. 11.

58. Ibid., p. 67.

59. Kazanjian, *Wizards of Wall Street*, p. 273.

60. Mitchell Y. Abolafia's ethnography of Wall Street examines community norms and collective self-restraint to place in context what would otherwise appear as the naked and unmediated pursuit of self-interest as markets get made not by individuals who surpass norms, but by social construction. See his *Making Markets: Opportunism and Restraint on Wall Street* (Cambridge, MA: Harvard University Press, 1996).

61. "The Slow Progress of Fast Wires," *The Economist*, February 17, 2001, pp. 57–59. In contrast, 95 percent of those on-line use e-mail. Both figures appear on p. 57.

62. Cox and Alm, *Myths of Rich and Poor*, p. 27.

63. Arthur Levitt, "Plain Talk About Online Investing," speech given at the National Press Club, May 4, 1999, http://www.sec.gov/news/speeches/spch274.htm (1/01).

64. David Futrelle, "Day-Traders Are Here to Stay," *Money*, March 2001, pp. 133–34.

65. Thomas J. Stanley and William D. Danko, *The Millionaire Next Door: The Surprising Secrets of America's Wealthy* (New York: Simon and Schuster, 2000), pp. 3–4.

66. Ibid., pp. 4–5.

67. Ibid., pp. 298–99.

68. Wendy W. Simmons, "Despite Recent Wave of Corporate Layoffs, Most Americans Not Worried About Losing Their Job," Gallup Organization Poll Release, January 31, 2001, http://www.gallup.com/poll/releases/pr010131.asp (2/01).

Chapter 2

1. Willard Stawski II, *Kids, Parents & Money: Teaching Personal Finance from Piggy Bank to Prom* (New York: John Wiley and Sons, 2000). Further page references given in parentheses.

2. David McCurrach, "Give 'Em an Allowance," p. 3, one of a series of articles on kids' allowances on the web site Kids' Money, http://kidsmoney.org/allart.htm#AmyN.

3. Elizabeth S. Lewin and Bernard Ryan, Jr., "How to Raise Money Smart Kids," *Consumers Digest*, vol. 16, no. 6, October/November 1995, p. 9.

4. Indiana Department of Financial Institutions, "Children and Money," http://www.dfi.state.in.us/uccc/CHILDREN.MON.htm.

5. Phil Laut, "Children and Money," *Inner Self Magazine*, n.d., p. 2, http://www.innerself.com/Parenting/Children_And_Money_by_Phil_Laut.htm.

6. David Owen, "Turning Childish Greed into Grown-up Capitalism," *Atlantic Monthly Online*, April 1998, http://www.theatlantic.com/issues/98apr/kidmoney.htm.

7. Carole Bozworth, "Teaching Children Money Habits for Life," http://outreach.missouri.edu/extensioninfoline/youth&family/money_habits4life.html.

8. Sharon Dawes and Tammy Dunrud, "Teaching Children Money Habits for Life," Children and Money Series, University of Minnesota Extension, 1997, p. 2, http://www.extension.umn.edu/distribution/youthdevelopment/DA6116.html.

9. Quoted in Janet Bamford, *Streetwise: A Guide for Teen Investors* (Princeton, NJ: Bloomberg Press, 2000), p. 8.

10. Michael Schroeder, Ruth Simon, and Aaron Elstein, "Teenage Trader Runs Afoul of SEC in Stock-Fraud Case," *Wall Street Journal*, September 21, 2000, p. C2, http://www.law.wfu.edu/courses/secreg-Palmiter/Handout/Articles/Schroeder-lebed.html.

11. Securities and Exchange Commission, Administrative Proceeding: File No. 3-10291, September 20, 2000, wysiwyg://8http://www.sec.gov/litigation/admin/33-7891.htm.

12. Michael Lewis, "Jonathan Lebed: Stock Manipulator, S.E.C. Nemesis—and 15," *The New York Times Magazine* (February 25, 2001), pp. 26–33, 46, 59, 66–67, 73. Michael Lewis, *Next: The Future Just Happened* (New York: W. W. Norton, 2001).

13. Richard H. Walker, "Regulation vs. Enforcement in an On-line World," October 25, 2000, p. 9, wysiwyg://11http://www.sec.gov/news/speech/spch413.htm. A piece by Daniel Kladec for *Time* magazine, "Crimes and Misdeminors: A teenager shows how easily stocks are manipulated and how hard it is to get away with it. So why are so many hailing him as a genius?" takes the same tack, October 2, 2000, vol. 156, no. 14, http://www.time.com/time/magazine/articles/0,3266,55712,00.html.

14. Yankelvich Organization for the Securities Industry Association, "Annual SIA Investor Survey: Investors' Attitudes Toward the Securities Industry, 2000," http://www.sia.com/publications/pdf/152000.pdf (5/02).

15. The self-help genre has been the subject of nuanced feminist criticism. See, for example, Elayne Rapping, *The Culture of Recovery: Making Sense of the Recovery Movement in Women's Lives* (Boston: Beacon Press, 1996), and Marguerite Babcock and Christine McKay, *Challenging Codependency: Feminist Critiques* (Toronto: University of Toronto Press, 1995).

16. From the back cover of David and Tom Gardner, *The Motley Fool Investment Guide: How the Fool Beats Wall Street's Wise Men and How You Can Too* (New York: Simon and Shuster, 2001). It is part of a trilogy. *The Motley Fool: You Have More Than You Think* and *The Motley Fool's Rule Breakers, Rule Makers* are the other two titles in the series.

17. These figures are taken from the Motley Fool site's tutorial on forming an investment club: http://www.fool.com/InvestmentClub/WhatIsAnInvestmentClub.htm.

18. Ken Little, *The Complete Idiot's Guide to Investing in Internet Stocks* (Indianapolis, IN: Macmillan USA, 2000). This cluster of quotes are all from the inside cover, n.p.

19. Data and information can be found at www.nasdr.com/statistics.asp#arbitration.

20. Jerry Mason, *Financial Fitness for Life: Advice from America's Top Financial Planning Program* (Chicago: Dearborn Financial, 1999).

21. Max H. Bazerman, *Smart Money Decisions: Why You Do What You Do with Money and How to Change for the Better* (New York: John Wiley and Sons, 1999), pp. 6–10.

22. Bill Schultheis, *The Coffeehouse Investor: How to Build Wealth, Ignore Wall Street and Get on With Your Life* (Atlanta, GA: Longstreet, 1998), p. 114.

23. Jerrold Mundis, *Making Peace with Money* (Kansas City, MO: Andrews McNeel, 1999), p. 247.

24. George Kinder, *Seven Stages of Money Maturity: Understanding the Spirit and Value of Money in Your Life* (New York: Dell, 1999), p. 21.

25. See, for example, Jacob Needleman, *Money and the Meaning of Life* (New York: Doubleday, 1994), and Jacob Needleman and others, *Money, Money, Money: The Search for Wealth and the Pursuit of Happiness* (Carlsbad, CA: Hayhouse, 1998).

26. Julia Cameron and Mark Bryan, *Money Drunk Money Sober: 90 Days to Financial Freedom* (New York: Ballantine, 1993), p. 199.

Chapter 3

1. Ulrich Beck, *World Risk Society* (Cambridge: Polity Press, 1999), p. 16. Beck's *Risk Society: Towards a New Modernity* (London: Sage, 1992) proposed a reflexive notion of self and society, that is, a self-awareness that

comes through making the world. Beck teamed with Anthony Giddens and Scott Lash to write *Reflexive Modernization: Politics, Tradition and Aesthetics in the Modern Social Order* (Cambridge: Polity Press, 1994), which treats reflexivity as characterizing a subsequent or "second" modernity. The breaks in modernity, which hold pride of place for rationalization that postmodern accounts would question, are also articulated in Giddens's *The Consequences of Modernity* (Cambridge: Polity, 1990). It is interesting that the literature on risk emerges at the same time as the phenomenon of financialization, which is treated as peripheral. This periodization of modernity reinforces the idea of a break between new and old social movements, the one based on knowledge and the other oriented to political economy. The distinction plays into "new labor" politics (in which Giddens figures centrally), whose electoral career has been based on the claim that it is not beholden to working-class formations like unions.

2. The distinction between risk and uncertainty is associated with Frank Knight; see his *Risk, Uncertainty and Profit* (New York: Augustus Kelley, 1964). Anthony Giddens has argued that the distinction can't be sustained conceptually. See Anthony Giddens and C. Pierson, *Conversations with Anthony Giddens: Making Sense of Modernity* (Cambridge: Polity Press, 1998).

3. Harry Markowitz is credited with the breakthrough quantification that lifts portfolio selection from intuition to science. See his "Portfolio Selection," *Journal of Finance*, vol. 7, no. 1 (March 1952), pp. 77–91.

4. On the culture and history of measurable information, see Mary Poovey, *A History of the Modern Fact: Problems of Knowledge in the Sciences of Wealth and Society* (Chicago: University of Chicago Press, 1998), and Theodore M. Porter, *Trust in Numbers: The Pursuit of Objectivity in Science and Public Life* (Princeton: Princeton University Press, 1995).

5. Despite the "new risks" like AIDS or global warming being hard to predict or cost because little is known about their trajectories, insurers can still securitize against population loss by hedging against a given incident. See Graciela Chichilnisky and Geoffrey Heal, "Catastrophe Futures: Financial Markets for Unknown Risks," pp. 120–40 in Graciela Chichilnisky, ed., *Markets, Information, and Uncertainty* (Cambridge: Cambridge University Press, 1999).

6. Dierdre Boden, "Worlds in Action: Information, Instantaneity, and Global Futures Trading," pp. 183–97 in Barbara Adam, Ulrich Beck, and Joost Van Loon, eds., *The Risk Society and Beyond: Critical Issues for Social Theory* (London: Sage, 2000), p. 195.

7. Niklas Luhmann, *Risk: A Sociological Theory* (New York: Aldine de Gruyter, 1993), p. 43.

8. Mary Douglas and Aaron Wildavsky, *Risk and Culture: An Essay on the Selection of Technical and Environmental Dangers* (Berkeley: University of California Press, 1983), pp. 7–8.

9. Herbert Simon, "A Behavioral Model of Rational Choice," *Quarterly Journal of Economics*, 99 (1955), pp. 99–118.

10. Peter Taylor-Gooby, "Risk and Welfare," pp. 1–18 in Peter Taylor-Gooby, ed., *Risk, Trust and Welfare* (London: Macmillan, 2000), p. 5.

11. Peter Lunt and Justine Blundell, "Public Understanding of Financial Risk: The Challenge of Regulation," pp. 114–30 in Taylor-Gooby, *Risk, Trust and Welfare*.

12. Deborah Lupton, *Risk* (London: Routledge, 1999), pp. 119–20. The Lash reference in the quote is to Scot Lash, "Reflexive Modernization: The Aesthetic Dimension," *Theory, Culture and Society*, 10 (1993), pp. 1–23.

13. The human capital framework has been developed by Chicago economist Gary Becker. See his *Human Capital: A Theoretical and Empirical Analysis with Special Reference to Education* (New York: Columbia University Press, 1964) and more recent *Social Economics: Market Behavior in a Social Environment* (Cambridge, MA: Harvard University Press, 2000).

14. A more general link between the symbolic and material resonances of risk as it is doubled in the domains of speculation and art can be found in Jean-Joseph Goux, "Values and Speculations: The Stock Exchange Paradigm," *Cultural Values*, vol. 1, no. 2 (1997), pp. 159–77. For a discussion of the development of risk out of the larger arc of modern dance technique, see Randy Martin, "Modern Dance and the American Century," pp. 203–26 in Townsend Ludington, ed., *A Modern Mosaic: Art and Modernism in the United States* (Chapel Hill: University of North Carolina Press, 2000).

15. See, for example, Mark Haynes Daniell, *World of Risk: Next Generation Strategy for a Volatile Era* (Singapore: John Wiley and Sons, 2000), p. 28.

16. See Bill Readings' discussion of the nonideological use of the idea of excellence in his *The University in Ruins* (Cambridge, MA: Harvard University Press, 1996), p. 24.

17. Dan Borge, *The Book of Risk* (New York: John Wiley and Sons, 2001), p. 207.

18. A fine generalist's account of the emergence of financial risk management is Peter L. Bernstein's *Against the Gods: The Remarkable Story of Risk* (New York: John Wiley and Sons, 1996). A bit more technical is Ron S. Dembo and Andrew Freeman, *Seeing Tomorrow: Rewriting the Rules of Risk* (New York: John Wiley and Sons, 1998).

19. Bruce Ackerman and Anne Alstott, *The Stakeholder Society* (New Haven: Yale University Press, 1999), p. 5.

20. Bernard Malkiel, *A Random Walk Down Wall Street*, 7th ed. (New York: Norton, 1999), p. 200.

21. The longitudinal evidence that investments with greater likelihood of varying beyond the market average yield greater return is provided by Roger G. Ibbotson and Rex A. Sinquefield, *Stocks, Bonds, Bills, and Inflation: Historical Returns* (Charlottesville, VA: University of Virginia, Financial Analysts Research Foundation, 1993), as cited in Malkiel, *A Random Walk*, pp. 204–5. Other studies, including Malkiel's own, have not found a relationship between return and measurable risk (Malkiel, *A Random Walk*, p. 230).

22. All figures were taken from graphs that accompany the article by Dave Pettit, "Still Clicking: Trading activity may be falling, but investors are still flocking to the Net. And brokerage firms are scrambling to give them what they want," *Wall Street Journal*, June 11, 2001, p. R4. The data also report that nearly two-thirds of on-line investors are male, and all but 7 percent have had some college education or more. In the first six months of 2001, investors averaged 9 trades each.

23. Figures taken from Daniel Gross, *Bull Run: Wall Street, the Democrats, and the New Politics of Personal Finance* (New York: Public Affairs, 2000), p. 6.

24. Cecily Fraser, "A Mood Elevator: Fed Cuts Marginally Lower Rates, But Boost Spirits," June 27, 2001, CBS MarketWatch, http://netscape5.marketwatch.com/news/story.asp?guid=%7B7B19E1D5%2D2 2FF%2D4CB4%2DABAE%2D9C1EDED872E1%7D&siteid=netscape (6/01).

25. Kevin Phillips, *Arrogant Capital: Washington, Wall Street, and the Frustration of American Politics* (Boston: Little, Brown, 1994). His books *Boiling Point: Republicans, Democrats, and the Decline of Middle-Class Prosperity* (New York: Random House, 1993) and *The Politics of Rich and Poor: Wealth and the American Electorate in the Reagan Aftermath* (New York: Random House, 1990) contrast sharply with his earlier *The Emerging Republican Majority* (Garden City, NY: Anchor Books, 1970).

26. Microsoft filing with SEC, "Management's Discussion and Analysis of 2000," p. 7, http://www.sec.gov/Archives/edgar/data/789019/000103221000001961/0001032210-00-001961-0006.txt (6/01).

27. Office of Investor Education and Assistance, SEC, *The Plain English Handbook: How to Create Clear SEC Disclosure Documents* (Washington, DC: SEC, 1998), p. 5.

28. Charlotte Cooney and Mary Lou Von Kaenel, "The Expanding Framework of Front Office Systems and Market Data Under STP and T + 1," June 8, 2001, p. 18. Paper downloaded from the Securities Industry Association site, www.sia.com.

29. Peter F. Drucker, *The Unseen Revolution: How Pension Fund Socialism Came to America* (New York: Harper and Row, 1976), p. 1.

30. Lawrence B. Glickman, *A Living Wage: American Workers and the Making of Consumer Society* (Ithaca, NY: Cornell University Press, 1997).

31. Damon Silvers, William Patterson, and J. W. Mason, "Challenging Wall Street's Conventional Wisdom: Defining a Worker-Owner View of Value," pp. 203–22 in Archon Fung, Tessa Hebb, and Joel Rogers, eds., *Working Capital: The Power of Labor's Pensions* (Ithaca, NY: Cornell University Press, 2001), p. 221.

32. Marleen O'Connor, "Labor's Role in the Shareholder Revolution," pp. 67–92 in Fung, Hebb, and Rogers, *Working Capital*, p. 80.

33. Eric Becker and Patrick McVeigh, "Social Funds in the United States: Their History, Financial Performance, and Social Impacts," pp. 44–66 in Fung, Hebb, and Rogers, *Working Capital*, p. 45.

34. Karl Marx, *Capital*, vol. 3: *The Process of Capitalist Production as a Whole* (New York: International Publishers, 1967), p. 436.

35. Leon T. Kendall and Michael J. Fishman, eds., *A Primer on Securitization* (Cambridge, MA: MIT Press, 1996), p. vii.

36. Leon T. Kendall, "Securitization: A New Era in American Finance," pp. 1–16 in Kendall and Fishman, *A Primer on Securitization*, p. 2.

37. Elizabeth L. Rives, ed., *Powering the Global Economy* (Securities Industry Association online briefing book, 2000), p. 12, http://www.sia.com/publications/pdf/BBchapter1.pdf (6/01).

38. For a précis and market information on REITs, the trade association, National Association of Real Estate Investment Trusts (NAREIT), has an extensive site at www.nareit.com.

39. IMF *World Financial Report*, December 1998, pp. 54–56.

40. Richard Minns, *The Cold War in Welfare: Stock Markets Versus Pensions* (London: Verso, 2001), p. 108. See also Robin Blackburn, *Banking on Death: The Uses and Misuses of Pension Funds* (London: Verso, 2002).

41. Elsewhere, I have sought to read Marx against these prevailing images of him, whether they be drawn by those friendly or hostile to his influence. See Randy Martin, *On Your Marx: Relinking Socialism and the Left* (Minneapolis: University of Minnesota Press, 2001).

Chapter 4

1. For an account of the move from Westphalian models of national currency sovereignty to the present configuration of interpenetrating national currencies, see Benjamin J. Cohen, *The Geography of Money* (Ithaca, NY: Cornell University Press, 1998).

2. For a trenchant examination of the Three Worlds history and concept, see Aijaz Ahmad, *In Theory* (London: Verso, 1992).

3. Shashua Chen and Martin Ravallion,"How Did the World's Poorest Fare in the 1990's?" 2000. Available on-line at http://www.worldbank.org/research/povmonitor/publications.htm. The authors identify regional increases in central Europe and sub-Saharan Africa, and a global increase in the $2-a-day rate.

4. I have discussed the use of tribalism as a global trope to do the ideological work of fear and loathing once performed by anticommunism in Randy Martin, "Resurfacing Socialism: Resisting the Appeals of Tribalism and Localism," Chapter 6 of my *On Your Marx*.

5. The estimate of global unemployment at 30 percent was made by the International Labor Organization (ILO) November 25, 1996, "Global Unemployment Crisis Wage Inequities Rising," on-line at www.ilo.org/public/english/bureau/inf/pr/96-40.htm.

6. In conventional accounts, it is economic implosion that leads to socialist collapse. David Kotz and Fred Weir show that the Russian economy was desiccated after Soviet governance ended. See their *Revolution from Above: The Demise of the Soviet System* (New York: Routledge, 1997).

7. In reflecting on the twenty years since the breakup of the Bretton Woods system in the early 1970s, Paul Krugman says of those who believed the new order would free the world from currency crises, "They were wrong." His own essays written in response to the ongoing crises make for a useful record and are compiled in his *Currencies and Crises* (Cambridge, MA: MIT Press, 1992).

8. William K. Tabb, *The Amoral Elephant: Globalization and the Struggle for Social Justice in the 21st Century* (New York: Monthly Review, 2001), p. 83.

9. William Jefferson Clinton, *Economic Report of the President Together with the Annual Report of the Council of Economic Advisers* (Washington, DC: Government Printing Office, 1999), p. 228.

10. The idea of the IMF as global safety net was promoted by Stanley Fischer, then number 2 at the fund. See his remarks, "On the Need for an International Lender of Last Resort," January 3, 1999, on-line at www.imf.org/external/hp/speeches/1999/010399/htm (1/99). For accounts of the new financial architecture and the Asian crisis, see also Barry Eichengreen, *Toward a New International Financial Architecture: A Practical Post-Asia Agenda* (Washington, DC: Institute for International Economics, 1999), and George Soros's argument that the crisis came from the structure of the financial system itself, in "The New Global Financial Architecture," pp. 86–92 in Will Hutton and Anthony Giddens, eds., *Global Capitalism* (New York: New Press, 2000).

11. International Monetary Fund, *Manual on Fiscal Transparency*, 1998, on-line at www.imf.org/external/np/fad/trans/manual (1/99).

12. International Monetary Fund, *World Economic Outlook and International Capital Markets: Interim Assessment*, December 1998, p. 57, on-line at www.imf.org/external/pubs/ft/weo/weo1298/pdf/pdf1 (1/99).

13. Basel Committee on Banking Supervision, "Bank's Interactions with Highly Leveraged Institutions," January 1999, www.bis.org/publ/bcbs45.htm (1/99).

14. A formative view was Roland Robertson's *Globalization* (London: Sage, 1992). See also Anthony Giddens, *A Runaway World: How Globalization Is Reshaping Our Lives* (New York: Routledge, 2000), and Ulrich Beck, *What Is Globalization?* (Cambridge, UK: Polity Press, 2000).

15. Lawrence Mishel, Jared Bernstein, and John Schmitt, *The State of Working America, 2000/2001* (Ithaca, NY: Cornell University Press, 2001), p. 288. Between 1979 and 1989, 13.6 percent of the population lived below official poverty rates, whereas between 1989 and 1999 the figure was 13.7 percent. Households headed by women are much more likely to be poor, and similarly, improvement slowed dramatically as such households became more common. In 1959 roughly 60 percent of female-headed households lived in poverty. By 1979 this figure had fallen to just under 40 percent. After increasing in the 1980s, by 1999 almost 36 percent of these households still fell below the poverty line (292). The trends in poverty rates are more useful than the rates themselves, which are used as benchmarks for benefits, and not a practical assessment that a family of four would be poverty-free if they made $17,000 or more in 1999. The poor worked longer hours and had less public assistance in the 1990s than previously.

16. Andrew Leyshon and Nigel Thrift, "Geographies of Financial Exclusion: Financial Abandonment in Britain and the United States," pp. 225–59 in their *MoneySpace: Geographies of Monetary Transformation* (London: Routledge, 1997), p. 228.

17. Michael Hudson, "The Poverty Industry," pp. 1–16 in Michael Hudson, ed., *Merchants of Misery: How Corporate America Profits from Poverty* (Monroe, ME: Common Courage Press, 1996), p. 2.

18. Eric Rorer, "Shark Bait: How Some Consumer-Finance Companies Make a Killing off People Who Badly Need Money," pp. 30–41 in Hudson, *Merchants of Misery*, p. 31. Rorer notes that in California between 1985 and 1993 the number of licenses issued for lending to those considered marginal credit risks rose from 1,942 to 5,008.

19. Mishel, Bernstein, and Schmitt, *The State of Working America*, p. 281.

20. For a critique of the development approach to thinking about the Third World, see Arturo Escobar, *Encountering Development: The Making and Unmaking of the Third World* (Princeton, NJ: Princeton University Press, 1995), and Colin Leys, *The Rise and Fall of Development Theory* (Bloomington: Indiana University Press, 1996).

21. The conference brought together representatives from governmental and nongovernmental organizations through a UN-sponsored event and a separate one for NGOs. The feminization of poverty spread by market economies is the principal source of obstacles to development, according to the NGO manifesto, which states, "We, NGO women of the world, rich in our diversity, have gathered along with governments in the largest global conference ever to address women's issues and the existing barriers to our achieving equality, development and peace. We believe that these goals can be realized by ending the oppression of women and girls, by women's full participation in national and international decision-making, and transforming the social, economic and political structures which underlie and perpetuate poverty, racism, inequality, injustice, unemployment, violence and war." Document on-line at http://www.igc.org/beijing/ngo/ngodec.html (7/01).

22. Stuart Rutherford, *The Poor and Their Money* (New York: Oxford University Press, 2000), p. 88.

23. Aminur Rahman, *Women and Microcredit in Rural Bangladesh: Anthropological Study of the Rhetoric and Realities of Grameen Bank Lending* (Boulder, CO: Westview Press, 1999), p. 149. Rahman's critique is at odds with many otherwise sunny accounts. See, for example, Helen Todd, *Women at the Center: Grameen Bank Borrowers After One Decade* (Boulder, CO: Westview Press, 1996), and Susan Holcombe, *Managing to Empower: The Grameen Bank's Experience of Poverty Alleviation* (London: Zed, 1995), who writes that the first "commandment" for managers that the Grameen experience teaches is that they "exercise tight, central control over the vision and values of the organization," 168.

24. For an overview of some expressions of microfinance internationally, see Maria Otero and Elisabeth Rhyne, *The New World of Microenterprise Finance: Building Financial Institutions for the Poor* (West Hartford, CT: Kumarian Press, 1994).

25. Quoted in Richard J. Barnet and John Cavanagh, *Global Dreams: Imperial Corporations and the New World Order* (New York: Touchstone Press, 1994), p. 383.

26. Lise Adams, Anna Awimbo, Nathanael Goldberg, and Cristina Sanchez, eds., *Empowering Women with Microcredit: 2000 Microcredit Summit Campaign Report*, http://www.microcreditsummit.org/campaigns/report00.html.

27. C. George Caffentzis, "The Fundamental Implications of the Debt Crisis for Social Reproduction in Africa," pp. 15–41 in Mariarosa Dalla Costa and Giovanna F. Dalla Costa, eds., *Paying the Price: Women and the Politics of International Economic Strategy* (London: Zed Books, 1995), as well as other contributions in this volume.

28. For a treatment of how risk tolerance differentiates the financial terrain among various global sites of poverty, see F. J. A. Bouman and Otto Hospes, *Financial Landscapes Reconstructed: The Fine Art of Mapping Development* (Boulder, CO: Westview Press, 1994).

29. For an overview, see Rae Lesser Blumberg, Cathy Rakowski, Irene Tinker, and Michael Monteon, eds., *Engendering Wealth and Well-being: Empowerment for Global Change* (Boulder, CO: Westview Press, 1995). Gayatri Chakravorty Spivak has identified what she terms "globe-girdling movements" as the primary political effect of the new formations, for example, in her essay "Supplementing Marxism," pp. 109–20 in Bernd Magnus and Stephen Cullenberg, eds., *Whither Marxism: Global Crises in International Perspective* (New York: Routledge, 1995).

30. The World Bank, *Entering the 21st Century: World Development Report, 1999/2000* (New York: Oxford University Press, 2000), p. 3. One example of a World Bank–funded project in Tanzania indicates its ambitions for microfinance to rationalize the natives and the national banking system, and enhance returns, all in one stroke: "The Rural and Micro-Financial Services Project will achieve quality, and, enhance the returns on governmental and donor's investments in the sector. In addition, related industrial skills will be enhanced, and a systematic tracking program will be instituted to analyze common criteria initiatives. Within the strategic context, the project will contribute widely to broad-based growth and poverty reduction, through the expansion of financial inter-mediation to small-scale rural and urban clients. The project components will include: 1) formulation and approval of a national micro-finance policy, to endorse international best practices, and direct the Government's activity in the sector, diffusing inappropriate political interference; 2) design of legal, regulatory, and, supervisory frameworks, focusing on institutional strengthening. Recommendations for revisions in the law and regulations will be developed, for final review by stakeholders; 3) preparation of operational guidelines, covering: banking; cooperative financial institutions; non-governmental organizations; and, capacity building initiatives; 4) institutional strengthening of the Bank of Tanzania, to improve coordination, monitoring/evaluation of micro-finance activities, and develop its Cooperative Department; and, 5) technical workshops/conferences, to enhance micro-finance knowledge and skills." On-line at http://www4.worldbank.org/sprojects/Project.asp?pid=P050441 (7/01).

31. For a revealing look at the case of Assam in the vise of Indian governmental antipathy and global human rights discourse, see Sanjib Baruah, *India Against Itself: Assam and the Politics of Nationality* (Philadelphia: University of Pennsylvania Press, 1999).

32. Some of the broader social entailments of new technologies are discussed in Manuel Castells's three-volume *The Information Age: Society, Economy and Culture* (Malden, MA: Blackwell Publishers, 1996–98); Mark Poster, *What's the Matter with the Internet?* (Minneapolis: University of Minnesota Press, 2001); and Patricia Ticineto Clough, *Autoaffection: Unconscious Thought in the Age of Teletechnology* (Minneapolis: University of Minnesota Press, 2000).

33. "Outlook 2000," *New York Times*, December 20, 1999, p. C21.

34. Even the idea of the Internet is beyond the reach of most Chinese ears. The venerable firm of George Gallup, employed to find out how many Chinese citizens had heard of the new technology, got an affirmative response from only 14 percent of respondents. Mark Landler, "An Internet Vision in Millions: China Start-ups Snare Capital as Auction Fever Boils Up," *New York Times*, December 23, 1999, pp. C1 and C4.

35. The forecasts come from the International Data Corporation, which bills itself as the "Global IT information resource" (at $1,500 per report), www.idc.com/AP112999PR.htm.

36. Elizabeth Rives, ed., *Powering the Global Economy: Securities Industry Briefing Book*, p. 14, http://www.sia.com/publications/pdf/BBchapter1.pdf.

37. William J. Mitchell, *E-topia: Urban Life Jim—But Not as We Know It* (Cambridge, MA: MIT Press, 1999), p. 155.

38. These are chapter titles from Jean Baudrillard, *The Consumer Society: Myths and Structures* (London: Sage, 1998). The visual display of goods as a substitute for direct participation is an argument made by Guy Debord in *Society of the Spectacle* (Detroit: Black and Red, 1983).

39. Rives, *Powering the Global Economy,* Chapter 3, "Savings and Investment," p. 43.

40. Bill Gates with Nathan Myhrvold and Peter Rinearson, *The Road Ahead* (New York: Viking, 1995), p. 182.

41. Bill Gates with Collins Hemingway, *Business @ the Speed of Thought: Using a Digital Nervous System* (New York: TimeWarner, 1999), p. xviii.

42. Material on Buffett, who has written no autobiographies or futurologies but has made plenty of public statements, is drawn from Andrew Kilpatrick, *Of Permanent Value: The Story of Warren Buffett* (New York: McGraw-Hill, 1998). Many kinds of shares are issued by Berkshire Hathaway; this is the priciest, cited on p. 834.

43. George Soros, *The Alchemy of Finance: Reading the Mind of the Market* (New York: John Wiley and Sons, 1987).

44. George Soros, *Underwriting Democracy* (New York: Free Press, 1991), p. xv.

45. George Soros, *Open Society: Reforming Global Capitalism* (New York: Public Affairs, 2000), p. 237.

46. The examples are from Stan Davis and Christopher Meyer, *Future Wealth* (Boston: Harvard Business School Press, 2000), pp. 21 and 47. The book is a brief for individual securitization as an image of replacing wage labor with selves valued as tradable commodities.

47. Robert J. Schiller, *Macro-Markets: Creating Institutions for Managing Society's Largest Economic Risks* (Oxford: Clarendon Press, 1993), p. 52.

48. Jeff Gates, *The Ownership Solution: Toward a Shared Capitalism for the 21st Century* (Reading, MA: Perseus Books, 1998), p. 295.

49. Rives, *Powering the Global Economy*, Chapter 4, "World Markets," p. 46.

Index